# THE POETRY
## OF FRANCISCO DE ALDANA

D. GARETH WALTERS

# THE POETRY OF FRANCISCO DE ALDANA

TAMESIS BOOKS LIMITED

LONDON

Colección Támesis
SERIE A - MONOGRAFIAS, CXXVIII

DISTRIBUTORS:

Spain:
Editorial Castalia,
Zurbano, 39,
28010 Madrid

United States and Canada:
Longwood Publishing Group,
27 South Main Street,
Wolfeboro, New Hampshire 03894, U.S.A.

Great Britain and rest of the world:
Grant and Cutler Ltd.,
55-57 Great Marlborough Street,
London W1V 2AY

ISBN.:84-599-2246-4
Depósito Legal: M-2071-1988.
Printed in Spain by Unigraf, S.A. Móstoles Madrid.

for
TAMESIS BOOKS LIMITED
LONDON

*In memory of my father,*
*David   John   Walters*

# CONTENTS

## CONTENTS

## PREFACE

*A recent and very welcome edition of Aldana's poetry — Poesías castellanas completas, ed. José Lara Garrido (Madrid: Cátedra, 1985) — appeared when this study had already been completed and submitted for publication. As the differences between this and the Clásicos Castellanos edition are slight, consisting almost entirely of orthography and punctuation, I felt it convenient to use the older edition as my source especially as it continues to be available. For poems not included in this edition I have adhered to the two-volume edition* (Obras Completas) — *effectively a reprint of the* princeps — *and presented the quotations as found. Although flawed and occasionally obscure this edition is preferred to the Cátedra edition for reasons other than mere convenience. I am not in full agreement with the solutions to poem-construction of fragmentary and incomplete compositions in the recent edition. Rather than embark on detailed textual controversies, which would have diverted me from my principal critical and analytic tasks, I have preferred to use as evidence the text of the* princeps. *My understanding of the poetry and my approach to the many incomplete and fragmentary compositions derive from the older editions and it is thus consistent that the quotations should conform to the same textual sources. This is not to detract from the many excellences of the Cátedra edition. Indeed, to assist the reader to refer to this and future editions of Aldana's verse I provide line-numbers in the case of quotations taken from the longer poems.*

*I am grateful to the University of Glasgow and to the Carnegie Trust for financial assistance towards the publication costs of this book; to the British Academy for a grant enabling me to consult editions of Aldana's poetry and other related material in Santander and Madrid in 1984; and to my wife, Christine, for her invaluable assistance in studying Italian texts of the* Cinquecento *and for her constant encouragement. In its embryonic form, this study took the shape of a lecture on tradition and originality in the poetry of Aldana delivered at the University of St. Andrews in 1980. For that opportunity and privilege I wish to express my gratitude to the Spanish Department of that University and, in particular, to Professor L. J. Woodward for his kind invitation.*

D. GARETH WALTERS

*Glasgow,*
*May, 1986.*

# INTRODUCTION

In 1939, the American Hispanist J. P. W. Crawford published an article entitled «Francisco de Aldana: A Neglected Poet of the Golden Age in Spain».[1] It could not be claimed, nearly half a century later, that Aldana has altogether emerged from obscurity, not, at least, to the extent of being as familiar and well-studied a figure as, say, contemporaries such as Herrera or Fray Luis de León. Admittedly, since Crawford's article, Aldana's works have been published twice: as a reprint of the original two-volume edition,[2] and in a more accessible and ordered edition,[3] but as the latter is in the nature of an anthology it does not include some of the important longer poems. Again, although biographical studies have yielded significant discoveries,[4] critical surveys of Aldana's poetry have been few and far between: only cursory attention has been paid to his verse, with the exception of two or three poems. British Hispanism has been unusually lacking in this respect for while respected scholars like Antonio Rodríguez-Moñino and Elias Rivers have striven on behalf of the poet, little has been published, even in article form, in this country. Indeed since the publication of two studies on Aldana's poetry in the early 1950s,[5] only one critic — Carlos Ruiz Silva — has taken it upon himself to subject the poet to the kind of scrutiny that his work demands.[6] But although this book represents an advance in the matter of breadth of coverage and close textual analysis, it does not endeavour to present a coherent picture. The author prefers to provide a series of partial glimpses rather than develop his material in accordance with a governing idea or a guiding thread; as its title states it is «studies» rather than «a study».

---

[1] In *Hispanic Review*, 7 (1939), 48-61.
[2] *Obras completas*, ed. MANUEL MORAGÓN MESTRE, 2 vols. (Madrid: CSIC, 1953).
[3] *Poesías*, ed. ELIAS L. RIVERS, Clásicos Castellanos (Madrid: Espasa-Calpe, 1957).
[4] ANTONIO RODRÍGUEZ-MOÑINO (ed.), Francisco de Aldana, *Epistolario poético completo* (Madrid: Turner, 1978), pp. 5-12; E. L. RIVERS, «New Biographical Data on Francisco de Aldana», *Romanic Review*, 44 (1953), 166-84. The former reiterates the mistaken suggestion, found in earlier studies of his on Aldana, that the poet was born in Valencia de Alcántara.
[5] ALFREDO LEFEBVRE, *La poesía del capitán Aldana (1537-1578)* (Concepción: Universidad de Concepción, 1953); E. L. RIVERS, *Francisco de Aldana, el Divino Capitán* (Badajoz: Institución de Servicios Culturales, 1955).
[6] CARLOS RUIZ SILVA, *Estudios sobre Francisco de Aldana* (Valladolid: Universidad de Valladolid, 1981).

Indeed in some respects it is disappointing that Ruiz Silva follows the same format as Rivers in his study: in both cases, biographical and bibliographical material precede the criticism of the poetry; and just as Rivers has separate sections on various genres such as sonnets and *canciones* so too does Ruiz Silva. Though the later critic pays generous attention to Aldana's sonnets in particular, he does so without any regard to such factors as possible chronology and development of themes. He is content to adhere to the slightly arbitrary ordering arrived at by Rivers and approaches the sonnets on a poem-by-poem basis.

As is so often the case with neglected authors, Aldana enjoyed a considerable reputation in his own day. There is a fleeting reference to him as early as 1564 in Gaspar Gil Polo's *Diana enamorada* and both Cervantes and Lope paid him glowing tributes.[7] Quevedo was sufficiently taken with his work to express the hope that, given time, he could produce a careful and corrected edition of his poetry in order to remedy the deficiencies of the first edition, prepared by the poet's brother, Cosme.[8] This is a task Quevedo would, in all probability, have discharged successfully to judge by his editions of Luis de León and Francisco de la Torre. In 1832, the American poet Henry Wadsworth Longfellow published an article on Aldana's devotional and moral poetry together with translations of some sonnets.[9] It is in the present century that Aldana has suffered neglect, at the very time when his contemporaries and successors, notably Góngora, have been revalued. Alone among the poets and poet-critics of the Generation of 1927, Luis Cernuda found the poetry of Aldana worthy of study and acclaim.[10]

Yet it might be objected that such a case as I am making reveals a critic's enthusiasm for his subject rather than the deficiencies of posterior judgement. Many poets praised in their day are indubitably not worth a second glance, while those ignored or even reviled during their lifetime have been shown, with hindsight, to have more to offer than their fêted contemporaries. This is true of all the arts. Nobody now asserts the superiority of Spohr's music over Beethoven's. But the case for Aldana does not rest on my taste and judgement alone. Despite its neglect, Aldana's poetry has commended itself very forcibly to those who have studied it, whether superficially or in detail. One characteristic claimed for his verse is originality and individuality. E. L. Rivers refers to its «variedad y... originalidad extraordinarias», and states how «es difícil relacionar a Aldana con otros

---

[7] Quoted in RIVERS, *Francisco de Aldana, el Divino Capitán*, pp. 133-35.

[8] Quevedo was particularly scathing about Cosme's edition: «Si alcanzo sosiego algún día bastante, pienso enmendar y corregir sus obras deste nuestro poeta español, tan agraviadas de la emprenta, tan ofendidas del desaliño de un su hermano que sólo quien de cortesía le creyere al que lo dice creerá lo que es.» *Anacreón*, XIX printed in *Obras completas. Obras en verso*, ed. LUIS ASTRANA MARÍN (Madrid: Aguilar, 1934), p. 668.

[9] «Spanish Devotional and Moral Poetry», *North American Review*, 34 (April, 1832).

[10] «Tres poetas metafísicos», *Bulletin of Spanish Studies*, 25 (1948), 109-18.

poetas, sean españoles o sean italianos». [11] This critic is, admittedly, a champion of Aldana's poetry and as such, perhaps, more disposed to scrutinize it for signs of distinctiveness. But when a history of literature makes the same claim, then it becomes especially significant. R. O. Jones refers to Aldana as «one of the most remarkable Spanish poets of the sixteenth century... [one who] strikes a very distinctive note in Spanish poetry of the period». [12]

On reflection, such statements are even more striking than they appear. To praise a poet for his originality may seem a standard kind of eulogy to the modern reader, but to make this claim on behalf of a Renaissance poet is far more unusual and significant. The rarity, if not the inappropriateness, of the concept of originality can be appreciated if I quote from the Introduction to a study of European literature of the sixteenth century:

> Originality in the sense of doing something completely new, and sincerity, in a simple autobiographical sense, are irrelevant concepts for most of the literature under discussion. Variations on a theme and the ability to express emotion within the strict conventions of style are Renaissance norms. [13]

As a more specific example, one could cite Bernard Gicovate's observations on Gutierre de Cetina:

> no es Cetina original en pensamiento o expresión; lo que lo coloca de lleno en su tiempo, puesto que el mismo concepto de originalidad era poco menos que inconcebible para el poeta del siglo xvi. [14]

What we are confronted with, then, it would seem, is a Spanish poet of the sixteenth century praised for qualities apparently at odds with what poetic theorists of that century valued most. This is the principal challenge posed by Aldana's poetry, nowhere more than in his love poetry. The priority granted to this part of his output in the following pages reflects an awareness of this fact. Furthermore, I believe that it is possible to trace the poet's gradual development from a standard mode of approach and expression to one that has earned him the reputation of individuality.

His background and formation mark him out as potentially different from other Spanish poets of his period — the first generation of Petrarchist poets in the Peninsula. Many Spanish poets from the fifteenth to the seventeenth century had connections with Italy that went beyond literary influence; the Spanish possessions of Sicily, Sardinia, Naples and Milan attracted, for

---

[11] *Poesías*, pp. xli; xlii.
[12] *A Literary History of Spain. The Golden Age: Prose and Poetry* (London: Ernest Benn, 1971), pp. 98-99.
[13] *The Continental Renaissance*, ed. A. J. KRAILSHEIMER (Harmondsworth: Penguin Books, 1971), p. 15.
[14] *Garcilaso y su escuela poética*, ed. BERNARD GICOVATE (Madrid: Taurus, 1983), p. 61.

various reasons, poets from the time of the Catalans, Jordi de Sant Jordi and Ausiàs March, through Garcilaso to Quevedo. But Aldana's links were particularly strong. He was born in the Spanish kingdom of Naples in 1537 of parents who originated from Extremadura, and he spent his formative years in Florence under the protection of Cosimo de Medici. Aldana's father was a professional soldier and military adviser and Francisco was to follow him in this career, distinguishing himself in campaigns in the Low Countries. He set foot in Spain for the first time in 1571, and only in 1576, when he was nearly forty, did he take up permanent residence, on his appointment as governor of the fortress of San Sebastian. His abilities as a military adviser led to his being appointed by King Sebastian of Portugal as one of his commanders in the ill-fated expedition against the Moors in North Africa in 1578, an enterprise about which Aldana had misgivings. His fears were justified: at the battle of Alcazarquivir, Aldana was killed together with Sebastian, and the Portuguese army was routed. [15]

Aldana was, then, the last of the soldier-poets who are so prominent in Spain in the middle decades of the sixteenth century. In his career he follows the example of many first generation Spanish Petrarchists; and in his death, that of Garcilaso who, forty years earlier, had also been killed on a foreign field. In other respects, however, not least poetically, we shall see how he differs from these writers. At the same time, it cannot be claimed that he falls readily into either of two new categories of poet: the scholar-poet exemplified by Herrera and the poet-cleric as seen in Fray Luis de León, although inevitably in his religious and philosophical verse he shares common ground with the latter. [16]

It is against such a pattern of vital and consolidating tradition that Aldana's achievement has to be assessed. What will emerge is evidence that in his finest poetry, whether amatory or moral, Aldana worked at the limits of experience and understanding. In him was an urge that drove him towards the extreme or the unknown. To ascribe this dimension — this transcendence of Petrarchist and Horatian values — to an interest in philosophy, deriving from the cultural milieu of his Florentine youth, can only be a partial explanation, although the Neoplatonic accent of his best-known love sonnets and of his verse-epistle to Arias Montano is clearly perceptible. There may be something to be said for ascribing his inventiveness to temperamental factors: Aldana reveals a trenchant, even rebellious, streak that perhaps marks him out as a suitable challenger of convention. But, in the final analysis, it is important not to underrate the technical or formal aspect. Just as the revolution effected by Boscán and Garcilaso was radically, or certainly

---

[15] For the fullest and most reliable account of Aldana's life see RIVERS, *Francisco de Aldana, el Divino Capitán*, pp. 9-123.

[16] It nonetheless seems to me misguided to include Aldana in an anthology of verse dedicated to Fray Luis and the so-called Salamanca school. See CRISTÓBAL CUEVAS, *Fray Luis de León y la escuela salmantina* (Madrid: Taurus, 1982), pp. 54-60.

initially, one of form and style, so too, arguably, much of the novelty and surprise we find in Aldana can be related to a willingness and a need to examine, probe and question the received terminology, formulae and structures and the attendant, nearly predictable, discourse. It is in these matters, at the very least, that we have a clear sight of the fruits of his much-praised individuality. My task is to discover the crucial moments of such potentially dynamic creativity.

# 1

## TEXT AND DATES

As with many Spanish poets of the Golden Age, the poetry of Aldana appeared posthumously. His brother Cosme published the verse in two volumes, the first (*Primera parte...*) in Milan in 1589, the second (*Segunda parte...*) in Madrid in 1591. The first part was reprinted in Madrid in 1593 (*Todas las obras...*) and with the 1591 edition it forms the first complete Madrid edition. To all intents and purposes, this is regarded as the *princeps*.[1] The only difference of note between the first parts of 1589 and 1593 is that the former concludes with an incomplete version (26 stanzas) of the long religious poem, the *Parto de la Virgen*. As this poem is printed in entirety at the start of the *Segunda parte* it is logically omitted from the 1593 first part. The two parts were also published separately in Flanders shortly afterwards and, as with the Madrid editions, the second part was the earlier. No date or place of publication was provided but from the evidence of the dedication to the Conde de Fuentes, Governor of the Low Countries, it seems likely that the Flemish edition appeared between 1593 and 1597 either in Antwerp or Brussels. The only novelty it contains is the inclusion of the *canción, A Cristo Crucificado* («Si al pie de vuestra cruz y a vos en ella»).[2] The Madrid editions were the ones chosen for the only modern edition of the complete verse *(Obras completas)*, but as this is a reprint rather than a critical edition it has resulted in a duplication rather than an eradication of the shortcomings of the *princeps*. Indeed other errors and misprints crept in.[3]

Editorial problems with Golden Age poetry are commonplace. There is scarcely a poet of note whose work does not yield sizeable problems of text or attribution. In the case of Aldana, the difficulties are even greater partly

---

[1] Fuller descriptions of these editions are given in the List of Works Consulted.

[2] *Poesías*, p. 33. Hereafter page-references to this edition are abbreviated thus: R, 33. In the case of successive references, the page-number alone is provided. Poems not included in this edition are taken mainly from *Obras completas*, 2 vols.

[3] For fuller details of the early editions, see RIVERS, *Francisco de Aldana, el Divino Capitán*, pp. 125-29.

due to his own neglect but mainly because Cosme was not the most competent of editors. The problems that arise are thus several.

One of these concerns the allegation of lost poems. At the end of the
*Segunda parte,* there appears a list of lost compositions.[4] If accurate, this
would comprise a large body of missing poems, but Cosme's claim has to
be taken seriously as he supplies specific titles or descriptions (e. g. «Obra
intitulada Cyprigna en dialogo, do fingia cierto retiramiento de Caualleros
en vida solitaria en la Isla de Cypro, en prosa y vario verso») and one poem
cited as missing has since been discovered.[5] Nonetheless, there are several
reasons why his claims should be treated with some caution. In the first
place, Aldana's output, though not large, is of a size roughly comparable
to that of other sixteenth-century soldier-poets like Garcilaso and Acuña. It
is possible too that some of the specified lost compositions are no more
than sketches or fragments as are a number of surviving poems. What seems
particularly open to question is the observation that a large number of un-
specified poems, written in the most common verse-forms of the period, are
missing: «Faltan infinitos Sonetos, Otauas, Canciones, y de todo genero de
verso, assi a lo espiritual, como a lo temporal de varias materias.» Other
Golden Age editors and publishers are prone to exaggerate when it comes
to lost works,[6] and it is possible that Cosme's «infinitos» is part of the same
tendency. Indeed, as we shall see below, a striking feature of Aldana's sonnets — his love sonnets above all — is their variety; it seems as if the poet
is loath to repeat himself. If there are a large number of missing sonnets,
then chance has been provident in allowing what looks like a representative
sample to have survived. But rather than believe in such a lucky coincidence,
I am persuaded more by the notion that Aldana did not repeat himself
because he was an experimenter, constantly on the look-out for novelty,
and not disposed to labour a theme or a formula. Finally, the suggestion
that Aldana himself destroyed some of his works shortly before his death,
probably out of religious scruples, seems to me ill-founded.[7] For if that

---

[4] *Obras completas,* vol. II, pp. 254-56. Subsequent references will appear thus: OC,
II, 254-56. With successive references I quote the page-number alone.

[5] The list of missing works includes «Vna obra de Angelica, y Medoro de inume-
rables otauas» (OC, II, 254). The poem came to light with J. M. BLECUA'S publication
of a manuscript of the University Library of Zaragoza: *Cancionero de 1628: Edición y
estudio del Cancionero 250-2 de la biblioteca universitaria de Zaragoza* (Madrid: CSIC,
1945), p. 326.

[6] Consider, for example, the seemingly extravagant claim made by PEDRO COELLO
in the dedication addressed to don Pedro Pacheco Girón to the *Enseñanza entrete-
nida i donairosa moralidad* (1648) regarding the number of lost poems by Quevedo.
This claim was repeated by GONZÁLEZ DE SALAS who, in the introduction to the first
edition of Quevedo's verse, *El Parnaso español* (1648), wrote: «No fue de veinte partes
una la que se salvó de aquellos versos, que conocieron muchos.» See J. M. BLECUA,
*Introducción* to *Obras completas I. Poesía original,* 2nd edn (Barcelona: Planeta, 1968),
pp. lxii-lxiv.

[7] See CUEVAS, *Fray Luis de León y la escuela salmantina,* p. 55.

were so, then surely those poems that refer directly and graphically to aspects of sexuality would not have escaped to the extent of forming one of the most conspicuous strands in the fabric of his total output. In brief, we would do well to presume that though some poems are missing, the loss is not of such dimensions as to render what has survived as anything less than representative. What we have is certainly sufficient to enable us to obtain a clear picture of a poetic personality and even to trace its development.

Incomplete poems pose another difficulty. Cosme suggests that 12 of the 68 compositions that appear in his two-volume edition are in some way unfinished, the omissions occurring mainly, as is to be expected, at the end of poems where such indications as «Aquí falta», «Faltan muchas», «Faltan innumerables» appear. In the majority of cases, it is clear that there is missing material but in others, the claim seems less valid. Such is the case with *Algunas otavas a lo pastoral*.[8] But a greater problem, as we shall see below, is that of the poetic sketches and fragments which figure in the hotchpotch of Cosme's editions alongside and with the same status as complete poems.

The principal commentators on Aldana's poetry, notably Rivers and Ruiz Silva, often refer to the obscurity or incomprehensibility of phrases or even whole passages. This is a feature that will be evident in a number of quotations from the poetry in subsequent chapters. To some extent this is again Cosme's fault as his editions provide abundant evidence of haste and neglect and a more conscientious editor may well have been able to iron out some of the problems, especially if he had had the advantages of access and acquaintanceship that Cosme enjoyed. In fairness to him, however, for once most of the responsibility must be laid upon Francisco's shoulders. There is little that an editor could do with such passages as the last *octava* of *Medoro y Angélica* with its obsessive punning on the word «paz»:

> La paz tomaste, ¡oh venturoso amante!,
> con dulce guerra en brazos de tu amiga;
> y aquella paz, mil veces que es bastante,      75
> nunca me fuera, en paz de mi fatiga:
> triste, no porque paz mi lengua cante
> (paz quieres inmortal, fiera enemiga),
> mas antes, contra amor de celo armada,
> huye la paz, que tanto al Cielo agrada.      80
>
> (R. 78)[9]

[8] See RIVERS, *Poesías*, p. 79n.
[9] Differing interpretations of this *octava* are provided by OTIS H. GREEN, «On Francisco de Aldana: Observations on Dr. Rivers' Study of 'El Divino Capitán'», *Hispanic Review*, 26 (1958), 117-35 (at pp. 119-20); and D. GARETH WALTERS, «On the Text, Source and Significance of Aldana's *Medoro y Angélica*», *Forum for Modern Language Studies*, 20 (1984), 17-29 (at pp. 26-27).

or such syntactically deficient writing as that found at the opening of the *Otavas en diversas materias*. I quote the first and third stanzas:

> Marte Dios del furor, de quien la Fama
> Por publico Pregon auia salido,
> Estar ardiendo de amorosa llama,
> Por la hermosa Madre de Cupido:
> Que esto assi se entendiò, porque en la cama       5
> Los vino a hallar el coxo su Marido,
> Y los cogio a los dos ambos desnudos
> En vna red de indissolubles ñudos...
> Ceñido de vna hembra al Dios furioso.
> Despues considera, por otro lado       10
> Estar qual Iauali fiero, y cerdoso,
> Que tiene al Perro en Monte acorralado:
> Tras esto el coxo andar muy querelloso,
> Venus corrida, Marte encarnizado,
> Con furia de Relampagos rodando,
> Los ojos que a Vulcano estan hablando.

(OC, I, 134-35)

Both the first part of the opening *octava* and the last part of the third lack a finite verb; the infinitives («estar ardiendo», «andar») seem grammatically unjustified and the relationship of the parts of the sentence, especially in the latter instance, is thus loose. The *Otavas*, admittedly, are an extreme case, as Ferraté has pointed out, [10] but such a tendency is by no means uncharacteristic. It may well have had the effect of deterring would-be editors.

Another inhibiting feature is the presentation and lay-out of the text both in the early Madrid editions and in the 1953 reprint. No attempt was made to organize the poems into any kind of grouping, either on the basis of form or theme. Worse still, on occasion the division between poems is not made as clearly as is usual, though even in this there is a lack of consistency. For instance on fols. 37r-38v of the first part of *Todas las obras*, four sonnets (*sonetos* I, XVIII, XIX, X), are printed without any intervening divisions, though inexplicably, a fifth sonnet is separated from the preceding block (*soneto* XIII). [11] On fol. 40v there is again no division between two sonnets (*sonetos* V and VI), but these are succeeded by a group of nine sonnets on fols. 40v-43v (*sonetos* XI, XII, XVII, VII, VIII, XXX, XX, IX, XXXII) where the separation of poems is clearly indicated. In this final instance, however, the lack of any effort at thematic organization is evident in the mingling of amatory and moral sonnets.

[10] JUAN FERRATÉ, «Una muestra de poesía extravagante (Las octavas sobre los 'Efectos de Amor' de Francisco de Aldana)», in *Dinámica de la poesía* (Barcelona: Seix Barral, 1968), pp. 215-23. The study is followed by a version of the poem with modernized orthography.
[11] The sonnets are identified by their numbering in *Poesías*.

More confusing still for the unprepared reader is the arrangement of the material on fols. 68r-70r of the 1591 edition, the second part of *Todas las obras*. On fol. 68 there begins a series of *octavas*. No title or heading is provided, however. The only indication of a new poem is a line drawn horizontally half-way across the page to separate the first *octava* from the preceding sonnet (*soneto* XXIX). Disconcertingly for the uninitiated, another dividing-line appears between the first and second *octavas* (still on fol. 68r). An understanding of such practices is only achieved if we have read the explanation contained in the title of another poem *(Otavas en diversas materias)* which appears on fol. 44r of the same part. In the end, the reader will deduce that the *octavas* that follow the sonnet on fol. 68r are not to be read as a single poem but as three poems or fragments of poems, the two horizontal lines marking the division between these fragments. The fact that the first fragment is but a single *octava* serves to confuse the issue even more.

Another instance of unclear presentation is provided by the two amatory *canciones* found between fols. 63v and 66r of the *Segunda Parte*. In the first place, the heading «Canción» seems to indicate that what follows is a single composition rather than two poems. Though there is an indication of missing material at what is in fact the end of the poem, we are not immediately aware that it is the end unless we are again appraised of the function of the «raya». Indeed until we pay close attention to the metrical form of the second *canción* we might be under the impression that the missing material occurs within rather than at the conclusion of a poem. What is confusing here is that though the stanza-length of the second *canción* is fourteen lines, each of the two stanzas that make up the poem is divided into two groups of eight and six lines respectively, and as the first *canción* comprises stanzas of eight lines, the reader could be misled at first sight. The use of the term «canciones» to refer to the stanzas of the first *canción* (a usage favoured by San Juan de la Cruz in his commentaries on his poems) is but a further contribution towards initial bewilderment.

Apart from incomplete works, there are among Aldana's output poems whose title or realization suggests that they are a grouping or collection of various poems rather than a single composition. Such is the case with the *Octavas* just considered (hereafter *Octavas sueltas*) and a longer set of *octavas* grouped under the title *Otavas en diversas materias*. In other cases, however, the work concerned is not as fragmentary or diverse as the title suggests. Such is the case with the *Otavas en diversa materia* (OC, II, 121) and the *Redondillas discontinuadas* (OC, II, 191), both of which, as we shall see, are single and complete poems. The set of *redondillas* headed quite simply «Otras» (OC, II, 194) comprises three poems. The second of these is a mere fragment of ten lines, while the first, a poem on two kinds of love — courtly and carnal — is reproduced in the Rivers anthology as *Copla* II (R, 141) and will occupy my attention in a later chapter.

11

The *Otavas en diversas materias* (OC, II, 134) consists of two kinds of material: a long poem that describes the effects of love by reference to figures of mythology and antiquity, and several brief fragments that between them amount to a mere eleven stanzas. While the former has received, by the standards of Aldana criticism, a reasonable amount of attention, the other fragments have provoked little comment. This is quite natural as they are neither complete enough nor good enough to warrant it. They are not without interest, however, for they provide an insight into Aldana's methods and interests. Some of these *octavas* give the impression of poetic exercise, while others may be no more than rejected material. For example, in the first of these fragments, the poet sets about defining love by means of opposites. He makes use of contradiction, paradox and oxymoron:

> Ardiente inuierno, elada Primauera,
> Dañosa caridad, bestial auiso,
> Pacifica discordia, y paz guerrera,
> Gozoso Infierno, y triste Parayso:
> Presente ya passado que se espera,
> Querer que no queriendo quiere, y quiso
> Incluye en si con largo laberinto
> Este aunque natural tan ciego instinto.
>     Pena, llanto, inquietud, ciego cuydado,
> Sobresalto, desden, facil engaño,
> Sospecha, ansia, temor, gozo turbado,
> Vil fé; salud incierta, y cierto daño:
> Lamentable reyr, temor osado,
> Contagioso mal nuevo, y estraño
> Es la infelice, y bien compuesta turba
> Desta Esphinge cruel, que el mundo turba.

(OC, II, 158-59)

There is in this section a parallel to an idea found in the principal poem of the *Otavas en diversas materias,* the so-called *Efectos de amor*: the description of love as «este aunque natural tan ciego instinto» harks back to (or anticipates) the notion of love as an overwhelming force —the principal subject of *Efectos de amor*. But the two *octavas* quoted above give an impression of jotting, a feeling underlined by the metrical awkwardness of some lines and by the weak rhyme at the end of the second *octava*. There is no indication here that this could lead anywhere; the intention seems to be to try out as many formulae based on opposition and contradiction as come to mind. But it is quite possible that as a result of such extensive scratching about the poet may have learnt the value of concision in the matter of Petrarchan antithesis, as witness the balanced and chiastic lines from the first stanza of *Medoro y Angélica* where he refers to the nature of the lovers' experience in these terms:

12

viven con fuego igual, con igual muerte:
verse la llama helar, arder el hielo...

(R. 75)

More evidence that Aldana sought in his finished, mature compositions a pithiness and a paring-down of standard Petrarchist formulae can be gleaned from comparing the periphrastic description of amatory tears in the following *octava* with the terseness revealed in some of his sonnets:

La terneza, y piedad que el vno siente,
Del otro al duro humor abre la via:
Della mil claras Perlas de Oriente
Salen, y della vn Tajo al Mar corria:
De las lagrimas del fertil creciente
Toma la della, y la que del salia,
Tanto es, que su principio saca, y mueue
Del liquido Cristal, que corre, y llueve.

(OC, II, 161)

Also present in these eleven *octavas* is a kind of amatory approach that, as the following chapters will show, Aldana did not favour or, at least, only cultivated in his least successful (and, I would argue, early) love poems. The following stanza is in a conventional pastoral vein, alien to the characteristic manner of the mature love poet:

Frisio pastor mançebo, cuyo canto,
Cuya apazible edad, cuya manera
Del Iauali cerdoso de Erimanto
El impetu, y furor domar pudiera:
Sirue, sigue, dessea, quiere, ama tanto
Lamia Ninfa del Tajo en su ribera,
Que no siento en amar tan alto grado,
Como dezir que amò quanto fue amado.

(OC, II, 160)

The one *octava* that above all suggests that these fragments should be interpreted as a kind of poet's workshop is the last of the *Otavas en diversas materias*:

En la cueua de Atlante humida, y fria
La soñolienta Noche reposaua,
Cinthia a su rubio hermano ya queria
Restituir la luz que del tomaua:
Todo en largo silencio parecia
Dormir, hecho insensible el mundo estaua,
En profunda quietud, y el ancho Cielo
Cubierto de vn escuro, y triste velo.

(OC, II, 162)

13

This is a description of the stillness of night in which myth is employed in a decorative fashion. The second stanza of *Medoro y Angélica* reads as follows:

> En la cueva de Atlante, húmeda y fría,
> la somnolienta Noche reposaba,                                  10
> y Cintia al rubio hermano ya quería
> restitüir la luz que dél tomaba;
> con el rosado manto abriendo el día
> la blanca Aurora flores derramaba,
> y los caballos del señor de Delo                                15
> hinchían de relinchos todo el cielo.

(R. 75)

The first half of the stanza to all intents and purposes duplicates what is found in the *Otavas en diversas materias* but the second part is completely re-written. It is almost certain that it is the passage in *Medoro y Angélica* that is the revision. There are differences both of subject-matter and intent. In the earlier fragment, the second part of the *octava* is a mere reiteration in more straightforward terms of the description of night. In the later poem, however, the corresponding portion of the *octava* describes the arrival of dawn and the rising of the sun. Moreover, the poet retains the mode of mythological allusion for the whole stanza, thereby combining development rather than repetition of subject-matter with uniformity rather than diversity of manner. The passage from *Medoro y Angélica* has an added significance because in the context of the whole poem the mythological descriptions can be seen to have an organic function: the eroticism of the poet's depiction of the lovers is anticipated in the terminology and phraseology of the second stanza. This is not only an elaborate account of night giving way to dawn but a reflection in nature and myth of the principal subject of the poem —the love-making and physical intimacy of the lovers. The erotic overtones of terms like «cueva», «abriendo», «derramaba» are supported by such ideas as the notion of virility in the image of the impatient, neighing horses and that of sexual giving and receiving in the description of the moon preparing to return its light to its brother, the sun. [12] This is a substantial advance on the single-stanza fragment but it is clearly there that the germ for the later poem is to be found.

Descriptions of nature figure prominently in the fragments of the *Otavas en diversas materias* and in the series of *Octavas sueltas* that appear later in the same volume (OC, II, 186). A favoured subject is the arrival of Spring and again a use of mythological allusion is prominent, as in the following stanza from the *Otavas en diversas materias*:

---

[12] These observations are drawn from D. GARETH WALTERS, «On the Text, Source and Significance of Aldana's *Medoro y Angélica*», pp. 21-22.

Mostraua el Sol con mas crecida rueda
A la mortal Region su cara de Oro,
Y visitar de la Tindaria Leda
Los hijos quiere, atras dexando al Toro:
El Ruyseñor cantando en la Alameda
Renueua al Tracio Rey su antiguo lloro,
Y sale a discurrir con libre buelo,
El circuyto azul del ancho Cielo.

(OC, II, 161-62)

In some of the stanzas from the *Octavas sueltas*, the poet expresses something of the same sense of wonder at the processes of nature as is to inspire the lofty eloquence of the *Carta para Arias Montano*. These two extracts do not remotely approach the standard of the verse epistle but they do show again perhaps the necessary apprenticeship. The seeds of the great vision are here:

Quien vee venir de rosas coronada
La Primauera con su Abril hermoso.
Tras ella el seco Estio, luego el ventoso
Otoño, y la sazon luego nevada:
Quien de mil nubes de Oro enguirnaldada
La Aurora vee partir del cano Esposo,
Y el rubio Dios con passo presuroso
Hazer luego tras ella su jornada?
Quien esto vee, que con vn O profundo
No exclame el hazedor de tan gran Mundo?

(OC, II, 186) [13]

No se si oydo aueis, que por el viento,
Por este espacio inmenso, y gran llanura,
Donde el aereo està claro elemento
Restaurador vital de la natura:
Por este que nos da vida, y aliento,
Por do nos lleua el Sol con su luz pura
La vista en peregrino, y facil buelo
Al de infinitos ojos rico cielo.

(OC, II, 187)

These two extracts do not belong to the same poem or projected poem but they have more in common with each other than do the first two *octavas* of the fragment of which the *octava* quoted above is the second stanza. In the first *octava* of this fragment, Aldana seems to be engaged in poetic jotting in a philosophic vein. The subject is the Platonic concept of

[13] M. LOUISE SALSTAD draws attention to the significance of circle imagery in this *décima* and relates it to Aldana's frequent use of the symbol of the sphere or circle for the Godhead. «Francisco de Aldana's Metamorphoses of the Circle», *Modern Language Review*, 74 (1979), 599-606 (at p. 605).

movement as it affects soul and body and the source may have been Chapter 15 of the Sixth Speech of Ficino's *Commentary*: [14]

> Alguno que alcançò, que no podia
> Vn cuerpo otro mouer, sin que el se mueua,
> Y vio que el mouimiento procedia
> De incorporeo poder que el cuerpo lleua:
> Vn ser que sin mouerse otro mouia,
> Y otro cuerpo despues hallò por prueua,
> Aunque era natural el mouimiento
> De la deidad de Amor hizo argumento.

> (OC, II, 186-87)

There is evidence that these fragments are early works. The *octava* that anticipates *Medoro y Angélica* may fairly be ascribed to an earlier rather than later period not only because of its mediocrity but also because *Medoro y Angélica* was in all likelihood not written in the last years of Aldana's life. [15] The third fragment of the *Octavas sueltas* is also an early work. It refers to a sea-battle between Spaniards and Moslems:

> Dentro el tierno Cristal mouible, y alto
> Mas intimo lugar del Oceano,
> Sintiose el graue son del fiero assalto
> Que de Meca al cultor dio el fuerte Hispano:
> Mouido pues del nueuo sobresalto                                5
> El humido Señor del Mar insano
> Las cristalinas sillas dexa, y viene
> Do nuestro ayre vital su region tiene.

> (OC, II, 188)

An allusion later in the poem to «El inmortal Garcia, raro caudillo» (1. 51) suggests a date shortly after 1564. In that year, Don García de Toledo, at the head of an expeditionary force consisting of Spaniards from the Italian colonies, captured the Peñón de Vélez de la Gomera.

More problematic is the case of the longest of all these fragments, the more or less complete poem, *Efectos de amor*. I have cited instances of sloppy

---

[14] «Every body is moved by something else, but no body is able to move of its own accord, since it is not able to do anything through itself. But because of the presence of the soul the body seems to be moved by itself, and because of the soul, to live. And, indeed, when the soul is present the body does move itself in a sense, but when the soul is absent, it is moved only by something else, because it does not possess this faculty of moving of itself.» *Marsilio Ficino's Commentary on Plato's* Symposium, translated by SEARS REYNOLDS JAYNE (Columbia: University of Missouri, 1944), p. 208. The passage also recalls Aristotle's theory of the prime mover, an argument employed by St Thomas Aquinas to prove the existence of God.

[15] MAXIME CHEVALIER, basing himself on Rivers' biography, suggests 1567 as a likely *terminus ad quem. Los temas ariostescos en el romancero y la poesía española del siglo de oro* (Madrid: Castalia, 1968), p. 303.

or deficient syntax in this poem but against that there are several passages of considerable poise and brilliance, notably in the section that retells the story of Jupiter and Europa (OC, II, 145-50). [16] Moreover, the concluding *octavas* of the poem enunciate a view of love that is akin, in expressive intensity as well as in thematic detail, to the mature love sonnets:

> En todo biue esta apegada Furia,
> Y todo en todo passa, y se transforma,
> Hasta en el Angel ay tanta luxuria
> De pegarse al Autor, por quien se informa:
> Natura contraher no puede injuria       525
> Si a la materia da su noble forma
> De quien recibe, y da la madre antigua
> Dulce, y eternamente vida amiga.
>    La qual por conseguir prenda segura
> Deste su proceder perpetuo, y biuo,       530
> Dio (Ved que gran saber) tanta dulçura
> Al impetu dulcissimo lasciuo,
> Haziendole (O de madre gran cordura)
> Tan dulce, como breue, y fugitivo,
> Porque aquel gusto a dar vida nos lleue,       535
> Y quede en el dador por ser tan breue.

(OC, II, 158)

We shall see the same notion of the irresistible force of sexual instinct in a poem like *soneto* XVII (R, 12), while the idea that the pleasures of love are fleeting receives a memorable treatment in *soneto* XII (R, 9). What is not present, or at least not explicit, in the sonnets is the relationship of the sexual urge to the reproductive one such as we find in the *octavas* quoted above, although in *Medoro y Angélica*, the poet-lover endeavours to justify his amatory aspiration by pointing to the lofty origins of his desire. It is seen as fulfilling a part of the divine scheme: «Gracia particular que el alto cielo / quiso otorgar al bajo mundo en suerte» (R, 75).

Another striking feature of the *Octavas en diversas materias* is the variety of register. Against the earnestness of the conclusion one can set the humour and irony of the approach in the opening tale of Mars, Venus and Vulcan. [17] In all, then, the poem does not reveal so much a lack of maturity as a lack of care. This makes it not only a difficult poem to study but one which, like many of Aldana's poems, is, at first sight at least, difficult to date.

The only poem of Aldana's published in his lifetime was a sonnet in Italian, *soneto* XXIII (R, 16), which takes the form of a reply to a sonnet by Varchi on the death in 1562 of doña Leonor de Toledo, Duchess of Florence and daughter of the Viceroy of Naples, don Pedro. Another son-

---

[16] See RUIZ SILVA, *Estudios sobre Francisco de Aldana*, pp. 174-76.
[17] J. M. Cossío concludes that most Golden Age poets viewed Vulcan as a figure of fun. *Fábulas mitológicas en España* (Madrid: Espasa-Calpe, 1952), p. 888.

net, again in Italian, on the death of Lucrecia, daughter of the Duke and Duchess of Florence, can be dated 1561 or very soon after. Though no other poems can be definitely ascribed to this early period, it is fairly certain that Aldana had established his reputation as a poet by the early 1560s in view of Varchi's reference to him as «pio poeta» in 1562, and Gil Polo's flattering mention of him in Book III of *Diana enamorada* (1564). Varchi's description indeed indicates that by 1562 Aldana had composed religious verse, including, in all probability, the poem in *octavas*, the *Parto de la Virgen* (OC, II, 37), which is an imitation of Sannazaro's *De Partu Virginis*. The other major translation, or imitation-translation, the *Fabula de Phaetonte* (OC, I, 147), based on Alamanni's *Favola di Faetonte*, [18] is probably also an early work as in his mature compositions Aldana shows little enthusiasm for imitation. It is likely too that by the early 1560s he had started writing love poetry, probably the more conventional courtly-Petrarchist poems, such as the sonnets to be discussed in the next chapter. [19] This possibility is confirmed by the fact that in a poem of 1568, the *Respuesta a Cosme de Aldana* (R, 48), the poet states that he had written poetry to Galatea, a name which, according to Cosme, refers to a Florentine lady. As she is the subject of some of Aldana's most passionate, unconventional and accomplished poetry, it is clear that the less adventurous and more standard form of amatory verse must predate the mid-1560s, probably by a number of years. This is an issue to which I shall return in the following chapter.

From the mid to late 1560s date three poems. The *Otavas sobre la vida retirada* (R, 88) was, according to Cosme, written while Francisco led an idyllic life in Florence, that is to say, before 1566. A verse epistle, the *Respuesta a Cosme de Aldana* (R, 48) bears a specific date —10 March 1568 (i. e. shortly after Francisco's arrival in the Low Countries)— while a shorter poem, again in epistolary form, *Pocos tercetos escritos a un amigo* (R, 55), addressed to an un-named friend, can on the basis of internal evidence be dated as late 1568. [20] What is significant about these three poems is their ready recourse to hyperbaton, often of a violent kind. In the *Otavas sobre la vida retirada,* we read:

---

[18] For a detailed analysis of Aldana's treatment of the fable and a comparison with both the Italian source and Ovidian original, see RUIZ SILVA, *Estudios sobre Francisco de Aldana*, pp. 147-70.

[19] In paying tribute to ALDANA in Book III of *Diana enamorada*, published in 1564, GIL POLO specifically compares him to PETRARCH:

> con gran razón los hombres señalados
> en gran duda pondrán, si él es Petrarca
> o si Petrarca es él...

*Diana enamorada*, ed. RAFAEL FERRERES (Madrid: Clásicos castellanos, 1962), p. 171. RIVERS thus reasonably deduces that Aldana's reputation by this date would have rested principally on his love poetry. *Francisco de Aldana, el Divino Capitán,* p. 133.

[20] See *Poesías,* p. 56n.

> Ciñe la frente del metal que al mundo
> desnudo al fin dejó del siglo de oro...                              10
>
> (R. 89)

This tendency is even more pronounced in the epistle to Cosme, as the opening lines reveal:

> En amigable estaba y dulce trato,
> trato amigable y dulce...
>
> (R. 48)

Fourteen lines below is a passage that contains a striking dislocation of noun from epithet:

> en esto el puro sale entendimiento,
> casi vestido sol de rayos de oro...
>
> (R. 49)

In another passage around line 40, the verb intrudes between a noun and its possessive:

> el impetu tal fué (¡ved lo que puede
> ardiente voluntad!), que allá en las celdas                         40
> más íntimas se entró de la memoria.
>
> (R. 50)

In the *Pocos tercetos escritos a un amigo,* the trend continues, as can be seen from the opening lines:

> Mientras estáis allá con tierno celo,
> de oro, de seda y púrpura cubriendo
> el de vuestra alma vil terrestre velo,
> sayo de hierro acá yo estoy vistiendo...
>
> (R. 55)

In view of the pronounced tendency towards hyperbaton in the poetry of this period —greater than in poems that can be definitely ascribed to an earlier or later period— there may be some justification for suggesting a date of 1565-70 for the principal poem (*Efectos de amor*) of the *Otavas en diversas materias.* The poem reveals the same ready recourse to extreme hyperbaton as for example in this passage which describes a horse in a state of sexual excitement:

> Se empina, se rebuelue, entrega al viento
> La sesga cola, y cerdas ondeadas,
> Saca del cuerpo vn caluroso aliento.

De sus dando señal llamas cerradas:
Cuyo furioso, y libre mouimiento                                    445
Despeñaderos, montes, ni quebradas,
De valle, rio profundo, o risco erguido
Iamas pudo enfrenar, ni ha detenido.

(OC, II, 154)

Though this is a later date than has hitherto been suggested for this poem, it is, I believe, a justifiable one in view of the high quality of some of the passages, as mentioned above.

The last years of Aldana's life again provide no more than a handful of datable poems. The sonnet dedicated to Philip II's fourth wife, Anne of Austria (R, 21), was written in or shortly after 1570, the year of her marriage to the Spanish King. A *terminus a quo* of 1571 applies to *soneto* XXVII (R, 20), addressed to Philip II and containing a flattering allusion to Don John of Austria, the victorious commander at Lepanto. The important political poem, again addressed to Philip II, the *Otavas dirigidas al rey don Felipe* (R, 101) dates probably from as late as the last year of Aldana's life; Rivers is of the view that it could not have been written before the poet's visit to Portugal in the summer of 1577.[21] The *Carta para Arias Montano* (R, 57) is another late poem. It bears the date 7 September 1577, and it may well be Aldana's swansong. More tentatively, a group of five sonnets (*sonetos* XXX-XXXIV) could be seen as belonging to the poet's last few years (R, 23-25); there are, in fact, clear parallels between some of them and the *Carta para Arias Montano*. This is a comparison I shall develop in the final chapter.

The late poems do not yield as many clear stylistic pointers as those from the late 1560s. It seems, though, that the poet's enthusiasm for hyperbaton had diminished, and, in the *Carta para Arias Montano* especially, that he favoured the simile, often an extended one. It would be rash, however, to view this as a new stylistic departure in Aldana's work and one cut short by his untimely death. It may be that the particular subject of the metaphysical, even mystical, *Carta* demanded a particular kind of rhetorical procedure, though, as we shall see in a later chapter, the poet uses figurative language, including the simile, in a telling way at the start of one of his love poems, the *Epístola a una dama cuyo principio falta* (R, 43). Perhaps all we can say about Aldana's use of the simile, then, is that he uses it sparingly or that he reserves it for a small number of his poems.

The evidence marshalled above is of varying degrees of reliability but it is sufficient to suggest an outline of the principal trends and stages in

---

[21] He sees evidence for this in COSME's dedication to the *Primera parte*, addressed to Philip II: «Aviendo mi hermano Francisco de Aldana (poco antes que le matassen peleando en la jornada de Africa) escritas de su propria mano, y dadas a V. Magestad ciertas octauas suyas, en materia de guerra» (OC, I, 5). See RIVERS, *Francisco de Aldana, el Divino Capitán*, p. 103.

Aldana's poetic development. On this basis, a number of poems, especially the longer ones, can be dated approximately, if not precisely. What this data fails to do, though, is to provide a guide to dating the sonnets, one of the most important and original parts of the poet's output. But in the case of the love sonnets, at least, the internal evidence is, I believe, helpful. A close examination reveals thematic and stylistic trends and differences — a matter that is pursued in the following chapter.

# 2

## LOVE POETRY (1) — THE EARLY POEMS:
## THE CONVENTIONAL APPROACH

The love poetry written in Spain in the century or so separating the first Italianate works of Boscán and the later poems of Quevedo has an uniform, it not predictable, quality. Admittedly the range of possibilities is dictated and limited by the vogue of Petrarchism and the ever-increasing recourse to Neoplatonic ideas, but these factors did not prevent the emergence of more distinctively original voices in other European countries: poets like Ronsard, Gaspara Stampa and Sidney, who view the literary amatory traditions with a more inventively questioning air. Even the advent of the *romance nuevo* in the later part of the sixteenth century does not produce any significant change of ethos in Spanish love poetry; far from inspiring a different view of love, for instance one that might correspond to the more varied and less courtly conception found in the popular and pseudopopular form of the *villancico,* the *romance* is, on the contrary, readily accommodated into the existing Italianate thematic mould. The *romances amorosos* of Quevedo, for example, occupy the same ground, thematically and emotionally, as the *canciones* and madrigals of the Italianate tradition.[1] This is not meant as a criticism of the poetry written in Spain during this period. Rather it is to imply that its merits have to be sought in nuances and slight variations of approach and rationalization within a well-established framework. Such poetry reveals considerable sensitivity and refinement by its painstaking attention to verbal and formal detail. In some respects, the coherence of ideology betrayed by Golden Age poets parallels the approach of the *cancionero* poets of the preceding century, and it might be wondered (though this is not the occasion to develop the notion) whether the lingering influence of the *cancionero* poets —at the very least as a literary experience for Golden Age poets— might be a factor in giving the love poetry of succeeding generations its homogenous appearance.

---

[1] See D. GARETH WALTERS, *Francisco de Quevedo, Love Poet* (Washington and Cardiff: CUA Press and University of Wales Press, 1985), p. 82.

The poetry of Garcilaso at the start of this period sets the tone. With light modifications the earnest lament of unrequited love continues through the poetry in Montemayor's *Diana,* the work of Herrera, Góngora's early sonnets, Lope's amatory ballads, Villamediana's sonnets and Quevedo's poems to Lisi. For all the modulations of detail and shifts of emphasis, the poetry runs along a single, well-ordered path. Symmetry —balance and contrast— predominates, not only in form but also in theme: the lover and the beloved, request and refusal, complaint and praise, lament and celebration.

Even from first impressions, the love poetry of Aldana strikingly does not conform to this pattern or model. What catches the eye immediately are poems that deal with love's fulfilment and the consequences of this. There are poems that variously celebrate carnal love, describe its limitations and, with the parting of lovers, regret its ephemeral nature. But although the standard amatory situation of Golden Age poetry is not a dominant, or even perhaps an obvious, mode in Aldana's output, there are compositions, nonetheless, that follow the conventional pattern arising from the fruitless quest for the remote, beautiful *amada.* What is remarkable too is that such a small body of verse should contain as many different perspectives on love, for the subjects of both fulfilled and frustrated love inspire varied realizations.

Though not numerous, Aldana's love poems are sufficient to enable distinctions, indeed divisions, to be made on a stylistic and thematic basis. In his edition, Rivers arranges the sonnets in an order which, together with other criteria, takes account of a possible chronology.[2] To some extent, his suggestions are acceptable, though he nowhere provides the evidence for his solutions. I believe, however, that it is possible to be far more specific in this matter. The clear stylistic differences, the divergent perspectives on the amatory experience and the different modes of rationalizing them are indicative of a gradual technical development. Furthermore, on this basis, there are grounds for dividing the love sonnets into two periods linked by a stage that is recognizably one of transition.

Although none of the love sonnets can be dated with any certainty, in one instance there is the suggestion of autobiographical allusion. This poem, however, needs to be treated warily. *Soneto* X (R, 8) is in fact a poem about friendship rather than love, though Rivers locates it among the love sonnets, presumably because the subject of friendship is developed by means of the pastoral convention and perhaps because the name of one of the shepherds, Damón, is frequently employed in the love poems. In his *soneto* XIV (R, 10), as we shall see, Aldana combines the themes of love and friendship in a particularly subtle manner, but *soneto* X is a mediocre piece:

[2] *Francisco de Aldana, el Divino Capitán,* p. 150.

Nuevo cielo mudar Niso quería
hacia los rayos de su luz primera
cuando lloroso y triste, a la ribera
de Arno, Damón su amigo le decía:
    «Sabe el Cielo, pastor, si juzgaría
por menor mal perder hato y ternera
y nunca ver sabrosa primavera
antes que ausente verte, el alma mía.
    Tus años goces, Niso, y sin cuidados
que descubran en ti vario accidente;
vivas alegre, venturoso y sano.»
    Esto dijo Damón cuando abrazados
los pechos se bañaron juntamente,
diciendo: «Adiós, amigo; adiós, hermano.»

The shepherd Niso bids farewell to his companion Damón on the banks of the River Arno. These circumstances invite a biographical approach: it might be wondered whether the leave-taking refers to Aldana's departure from Florence (hence the allusion to the Arno) to the Low Countries in 1567.[3] Aldana would already have written one poem on friendship and his idyllic existence in Florence prior to this date, the *Otavas sobre la vida retirada*. There may also be some support for a biographical interpretation of the sonnet in the shape of Damon's expression of concern at his friend's well-being in the first tercet. This might have been prompted by the knowledge of the dangers of the soldier's life to which Aldana was to be exposed more than previously and which he articulates via the *persona* of Damón. This would be a questionable interpretation, however. The main drawback concerns the straightforward nature of the poem: its uninspired, matter-of-fact tone. Syntactically and structurally it is far less intricate than many of Aldana's love sonnets, and to postulate a dating as late as 1567 would be to place it among the later amatory compositions, a proposition that seems particularly unlikely when it is set alongside the two sonnets that precede it in the Rivers edition (R, 7). These deal with conventional themes in an imaginative, even extravagant fashion, far removed from the direct, uncomplicated approach of *soneto* X. Moreover this sonnet reveals nothing of the violent hyperbaton present in the two preceding sonnets and which was a conspicuous feature of the *Otavas sobre la vida retirada,* written in or shortly before 1566, and the *Respuesta a Cosme* of early 1568. If any comparable biographical dimension is present in the sonnet, then, it seems likely that it would have to refer to an earlier departure, perhaps prior to the expedition before the battle of St Quentin in 1557 or with Aldana's appointment as lieutenant to his father at the fortress of San Miniato in 1563. It may of course refer to a departure of which we have no record.

---

[3] ALFREDO LEFEBVRE (*La poesía del capitán Aldana,* pp. 44-45) suggests that both this sonnet and *soneto* XVIII («¿Ya te vas, Tirsis?») were written on the occasion of the poet's departure for Flanders.

It is also possible that the poem refers not to a journey by Aldana but to one by a friend of his, as Damón is the name most often used as Aldana's *persona* and it is not Damón but Niso who is about to leave. In short, it is clear that little firm biographical substance can be extracted from the sonnet. On the other hand, there is a case for ascribing it to an early period on account of its stylistic and expressive character. Such an impression is confirmed when the sonnet is read alongside others which demonstrably constitute a group of straightforward, conventional and unambitious poems. Indeed it would be no exaggeration, in my opinion, to regard this group as belonging to an early, if not the first, period in Aldana's literary career. The stylistic and thematic traits of these poems are evidence of this.

I turn initially to those sonnets in which the poet adopts the classic role of the lover in the Renaissance lyric. The atmosphere in *soneto* XI is one of neo-pagan pastoral. The poet-shepherd addresses Venus and performs a sacrifice in her honour in order to win over his beloved:

> Alma Venus gentil, que al tierno arquero
> hijo puedes llamar, y el niño amado
> madre puede llamarte, encadenado
> al cuello alabastrino el brazo fiero:
> yo, tu siervo Damón, pobre cabrero,
> más no pudiendo dar de mi ganado,
> a tus aras y altar santo y sagrado
> ofrezco el corazón deste cordero;
> en memoria del cual, benigna diosa,
> por el Amor te pido, y juntamente
> pedirte quiero, Amor, por Venus tuya,
> que el pecho helado y frío de mi hermosa
> pastora enciendas todo en llama ardiente
> tal que su curso enfrene y más no huya.
>
> (R, 9)

Such poems are quite common in *seicento* verse and Fucilla has suggested two possible sources for this sonnet: Varchi's «Santa madre d'Amor, che inherbi e infiori» and Petronio Barbati's «Diva, che Cipro reggi almo e vezzoso». [4] Varchi's sonnet was freely translated into Spanish by Francisco de la Torre but it is more likely that Aldana would have known the original rather than the translated version as Varchi was his friend and mentor. [5] Aldana's opening also bears a resemblance to the first phrase of one of the best-known sonnets of Camões: «Alma minha gentil, que te partiste». [6] Al-

[4] J. G. FUCILLA, *Estudios sobre el petrarquismo en España* (Madrid: Consejo Superior de Investigaciones Científicas, 1960), pp. 158-59.
[5] Both these sonnets are printed in FRANCISCO DE LA TORRE, *Poesías*, ed. ALONSO ZAMORA VICENTE, Clásicos Castellanos (Madrid: Espasa-Calpe, 1969), pp. 55-56. RUIZ SILVA, however, expresses reservations about the suggested sources. *Estudios sobre Francisco de Aldana*, p. 72.
[6] See his *Obras completas*, ed. HERNÂNI CIDADE, vol. I, 3rd edn (Lisbon: Sá da Costa, 1962), p. 213.

dana's sonnet is far from being one of his best and shares some of the characteristics of *soneto* X: an unadventurous approach to structure and syntax, shown by the four-square presentation and the avoidance of hyperbaton. The adjectivization leaves much to be desired especially as in such straightforward, «classical» sonnets, lexical detail becomes an important, even crucial, factor as Garcilaso realized.[7] But Aldana's use of epithets in this sonnet is unimpressive and repetitive («santo y sagrado»; «helado y frío»), while the tendency to repetition is seen in other ways in the sonnet: in the synonymous «tus aras y altar», and in the ungainly circumlocution of «por el Amor te pido, y juntamente / pedirte quiero» —a mannerism of *cancionero* poetry of a kind to which Aldana too readily succumbed. Nonetheless, I feel that Fucilla's view of the sonnet as mediocre, echoed by Ruiz Silva's assessment of it as «de muy inferior calidad», to be unduly harsh.[8] The poem has touches of concentration and density that the sonnets of Varchi and Francisco de la Torre lack. The description of Cupid embracing Venus in the first quatrain is a fine realization of movement and visual vividness. There is, furthermore, an ironic contrast implied between the tenderness of this embrace and the lover's failure in his pursuit of his disdainful shepherdess —a parallel underscored by the phrase «cuello alabastrino» which is used here to describe Venus but which is a standard term in the Petrarchist portrait of the beloved. The conclusion of the sonnet provides another neat feature. The poet plays conventionally on the Petrarchist oxymoron of the icy fire, but the conceit is thought through and at the same time concise so that the ending is a crisp one. This effect is enhanced by the variety of pace and rhythm in the final tercet. The smoothness and euphony of the first two lines, linked by a pronounced *enjambement,* contrasts with the slightly stuttering abruptness of the last half-line. The poet asks that the ice of his beloved's disdain be thawed by the fire of his passion and (developing the conceit) that the resultant water —a symbol of fertility and his fulfilment— should not elude him. This latter idea is reminiscent of a passage from Garcilaso's Eclogue I in which Salicio recounts his dream.[9]

---

[7] Consider, for example, the attention paid to the epithets in Garcilaso's *soneto* XXIII («En tanto que de rosa y azucena»), notably in such phrases as «vuestro mirar, ardiente, honesto» and «el hermoso cuello blanco, enhiesto». *Poesías castellanas completas,* ed. E. L. Rivers, 2nd edn (Madrid: Castalia, 1972), p. 59.

[8] *Estudios sobre Francisco de Aldana*, p. 97.

[9] Cf.

> Soñaba que en el tiempo del estío
> llevaba, por pasar allí la siesta,
> a abrevar en el Tajo mi ganado;
> y después de llegado,
> sin saber de cuál arte,
> por desusada parte
> y por nuevo camino el agua s'iba;
> ardiendo yo con la calor estiva,
> el curso enajenado iba siguiendo
> del agua fugitiva.

> (*Ed cit.,* p. 123)

But overall the sonnet is a light piece. It is a poem that neither reflects nor seeks to engender a profound emotional experience, unlike the later sonnets on love's fulfilment. Indeed, it might be suspected that it is this playful attitude rather than any technical deficiency that has prompted the adverse reactions. But such a light, even frivolous, approach is usual when Aldana writes about the standard amatory relationship and the sufferings of the lover. His more intense and personal utterances are reserved for different amatory situations.

A poem that illustrates Aldana's inability to rise above a level of mere competence when he deals with the theme of amatory suffering is *soneto* I:

> Si nunca, del umbroso y cavo seno
> saliendo con tu Flora mano a mano,
> Céfiro, viste en monte, en prado, en llano
> gozar el campo, de tu nombre lleno,
>
>    desecha ya, por Dios, del mar Tirreno,
> si tus orejas hiere el son humano,
> un movimiento crudo y tan insano
> que el Noto levantó por caso ajeno;
>
>    hinche las blancas velas, con las ondas
> menos hinchadas ya, del favorable
> y dulce soplo do mi bien consiste.
>
>    Razón es, santo Dios, que al fin respondas,
> pues mi plegaria justa y miserable
> contiene la razón que en ella viste.
>
>                                         (R, 3)

This sonnet also meets with Ruiz Silva's disapproval and in this case it has to be admitted that it is justified: the poem has few, if any, redeeming features. [10] It is an elaborate expression of the indignant poet's hope that his plea for the fulfilment of his love («mi plegaria justa y miserable») should be answered. But this elaboration is deceptive, serving only to cloak the poverty of idea and inspiration. The quatrains comprise a sprawling sentence that gives an impression of fussiness rather than structural purpose. The analogy between nature and the poet's emotional condition is essentially straightforward but the convolutions of syntax give a false impression of complexity. Indeed the signifiers (the gentle south wind and the stormy northerly) all but swamp the signified (the amatory contrast and complaint), and the lameness of the conclusion is all the more glaring because of the earlier decoration. In this poem, moreover, it seems as if the poet is under the impression that mythological and classical allusion must involve a portentous manner. What it signally fails to evoke is an insight into or even an understanding of unhappy love; that is rendered incidental, not essential.

Aldana was, fortunately, capable of better things even when writing of the conventional amatory situation. This is borne out by his *soneto* VIII,

---

[10] *Estudios sobre Francisco de Aldana*, p. 86.

an accomplished piece that probably belongs to a later period than the two
sonnets previously considered:

> Crudas y heladas ondas fugitivas
> que de mi bien la calidad hurtastes
> cuando el hermoso pie ledas bañastes
> al mayor sol entre mil piedras vivas:
>    así tan alta suerte, ondas esquivas,
> como ésta, que mi luz vistes y amastes,
> nunca os deje de honrar, pues le abrazastes,
> y siempre andéis de tal suceso altivas,
>    que, si de nuevo aquí volviere y ella
> pisare algún peñasco helado y frío,
> muy paso le digáis desta manera:
>    «A ti misma te pisas, ninfa bella,
> pues yo la hierba en mis riberas crío,
> y matas tú quien honra a mi ribera.»

(R, 7)

Several Petrarchist ploys are used with some success. The conventional hyperbole (1.4) is enhanced by the identification of the stream with the lady
(«Crudas y heladas»; «esquivas») and by the energetic working of a jealousy
conceit («vistes... amastes... abrazastes») suggestive of various stages of
love. But once again a desire for intricacy gets the better of the poet and
the conclusion is vitiated by its over-cleverness and obscurity. The poet asks
the stream to address his lady. This involves the conceit whereby she is equat-
ed with the icy cold boulder, but the concluding lines provide difficulties
of interpretation. The waters of the stream help the grass to thrive; by contrast, the lady is an agent of destruction. It is not clear, though, what «quien»
refers to. Is it the lady herself as she treads on the floor of the stream («A
ti misma te pisas»), in which case her beauty would honour, that is, confer
dignity on, the riverbank? Or is it the poet himself, who is «killed» (i. e. de-
jected) by his beloved's disdain and who, nonetheless, honours, that is, re-
veres, the bank because she has trodden there? Or, least likely, does it refer
to the grass, a symbol of the poet's hope? Ambiguity is not always a virtue
in poetry, and it cannot be said that it adds to the quality of the sonnet
after its purposeful opening. What is significant again, though, is the poem's
frivolity not to say irresponsibility. The wilful intricacy of the ending serves
only to deprive the poem of its potential integrity, intellectual as well as
emotional. Such a procedure is quite different to the function of the conceit
in poets such as Góngora and Quevedo where the aim is intensification,
not dissipation as here. This sonnet provides more evidence of Aldana's tendency to associate the conventional courtly lament with a brand of witty
Petrarchism characterized by cleverness and extravagance, and seemingly
to reserve the commonest of Renaissance amatory attitudes for such frivolous or occasional poems.

The praise of the lady's beauty is a common subject in Petrarchist poetry and often serves as an antithesis to the lover's lament: the light of her beauty contrasts with and may alleviate his emotional darkness. With the ever-increasing recourse to Neoplatonic concepts, the topic of beauty inspires poems of a lofty and ethereal quality as witness the hymn-like utterances of Herrera and Villamediana. For Aldana, however, the theme does not arouse such commitment or devotion. As with the subject of suffering, his approach is, at worst, shallow, at best, merely playful:

> Esta es la mano alabastrina, y bella
> Per cui spari dal Cor lo antico gelo;
> Esta es la mano Amor, que biue en ella
> Quato [sic] ha di bel l'alma Natura, e'l Cielo:
> Otra no puede ser, si esta no es ella,      5
> Che opra ne l'Alma il duol che si mal celo:
> Si esta es la mano, que mi mano aprieta
> Vendetta Amor, ahy giusto Amor vendetta.
>    Esta es la mano Angelica, y diuina,
> Pace del viuer mio, che in terra adoro:      10
> Esta es la mano Amor, que sola es dina
> Di esser eletta nel sublime choro:
> Esta es la mano Amor, que medecina
> E di quel duol percui languisco, e moro,
> Si en esta mano està mi muerte, y vida      15
> Vendetta Amor del mal ch'in me si annida.

(OC, II, 213)

Beauty is the subject for this poetic exercise of alternating Spanish and Italian lines, in all likelihood an early work as most of the small number of Aldana's Italian poems have been definitely dated as early compositions. These *octavas* are in the tradition of Petrarchist poems that focus on a single attribute of the lady's beauty and which are content to confine themselves to a series of varying descriptions of and responses to that particular attribute. [11] The poem is untypical of Aldana in one important respect: the emphasis in his description of the lady's hand on a spiritual understanding of beauty —a rationalization that progresses from the initial visual or physical apprehension («mano alabastrina») to a lofty, ethereal one («la mano... dina / Di esser eletta nel sublime choro»). Such a Platonic process, even in as light a vein as this, is generally absent from Aldana's love poetry, though it is common enough in the work of his contemporary, Herrera. Perhaps the experience of composing verses in Italian, if only for half the poem, unconsciously led Aldana into such an appraisal. The outcome is a poem of a little charm but no weight — one that provides an unmistakable impression of second-hand emotion.

[11] See LEONARD FORSTER, *The Icy Fire. Five Studies in European Petrarchism* (Cambridge: Cambridge University Press, 1969), p. 10.

But this poem seems positively inspired when set alongside the two-stanza poem entitled vaguely *Otavas sueltas del autor*. The opening *octava* should suffice as an illustration of some of the most banal lines Aldana ever penned, even allowing for the fact that it might have been only a sketch. This would be poor quality even for first thoughts:

> Eres mas blanca, y bella mi Pastora,
> Que blanca, y bella Rosa en verde Mayo,
> Mas dulce, y tierna que vital Aurora,
> Denunciadora al Sol del claro Rayo.
> Y para el que te sirue, ama, y adora      5
> Mas fria, y muerta, que el mortal desmayo
> De mi adorada, amada, y mas querida,
> Que Choça, Haro, Bareña, y que la vida.

(OC, I, 229)

It is not just that the diction is limited and repetitive, the metaphors hackneyed, and the phraseology rendered stilted by the repeated binary formula. There are rudimentary technical flaws too: a weak rhyme («Mayo», «desmayo») and awkwardly-constructed hendecasyllables, the fifth and eighth lines particularly.

Such a poem is rare, if not unique, in Aldana's output. Though seldom inspired by the idea of the lady's beauty — *Medoro y Angélica* is an exception — he was, at least, on most occasions capable of competence. Such is the case with *soneto* III, in all probability an early work:

> Hase movido, dama, una pasión
> entre Venus, Amor y la Natura
> sobre vuestra hermosísima figura,
> en la cual todos tres tienen razón.
>    Buscan quien les absuelva esta quistión
> con viva diligencia y suma cura,
> y es tan alta, tan honda y tan oscura
> que no hay quien dalle pueda solución.
>    Ponen estas querellas contra vos:
> Venus, que le usurpáis su sacrificio;
> Amor, que no lo conocéis por dios;
>    Natura dice y jura por su oficio
> que de vuestra impresión nunca hizo dos
> y que ingrata le sois del beneficio.

(R, 4)

The structure is straightforward: the formal divisions of the sonnet correspond to the stages of the poet's discourse or argument. It has none of the syntactical adventure or the experimental and innovative touches (e. g. the use of dialogue) of other, later sonnets. This regular or «classical» sonnet-structure is not a drawback in itself as some of the earlier Spanish Petrarchists demonstrated, but it requires a compensating verbal or conceptual

30

dynamism and neither of these is in evidence here. What could have been poise and restraint instead becomes flatness and stasis. The periphrases and circumlocutions of lines 6, 7 and 12 seem merely to mark time, while the summing-up is unimaginatively rendered by the persistent use of the «que» clause. As a consequence, by this four-square realization, the final conceit —the idea that the beloved's beauties duplicate and make redundant the beauties of the natural world— is made to seem all the more commonplace. Here, however, it is not so much a matter of technical shortcoming as a failure adequately to respond to a standard topic.

A more interesting attempt at treating the theme of the lady's beauty is to be found in *soneto* V. As with *soneto* VIII, where Aldana comes to grips quite successfully with the topos of the beloved's cruelty, the vehicle of the occasional sonnet serves to raise the level of intellectual and imaginative commitment. The poem is built upon the poet's reaction to a scene in which a beautiful woman has been struck a blow by a man, as a result of which her beauty is momentarily hidden from the poet's gaze. We are not told who the protagonists are, nor informed as to the relationship between them. The poem is shaped, even contrived, so as to maximize its witty potential. For all that, it has a verve that *soneto* III lacks, even if the indignation is forced:

> ¡Oh mano convertida en duro hielo,
> turbadora mortal de mi alegría!,
> ¿podiste, mano, escurecer mi día,
> turbar mi paz, robar su luz al cielo?
> El rubio dios que nos alumbra el suelo
> corre con más placer que antes solía,
> cubierta viendo a quien su luz vencía
> de un mal causado, indino y turbio velo.
> ¡Goza, invidiosa luz, goza de aquesto,
> goza de aqueste daño, oh luz avara,
> oh luz ante mi luz breve y escasa!
> Que aun pienso ver, y créeme, luz, muy presto
> cual antes a mi luz serena y clara,
> y entonces me dirás, luz, lo que pasa.
>
> (R, 5) [12]

The first line provides a characteristically neat and ironic touch: the hand that dealt the blow is described as «duro hielo» — a metaphor that is often employed to refer to the whiteness of the lady's skin, frequently her hand. The double and contrasting associations of ice in this case — between what

---

[12] A similar subject is treated by LOPE DE VEGA in his sonnet «Para que no compréis artificiales». This is a more ostensibly burlesque poem than Aldana's, although it makes use of similar conceits («¿Herir al sol en medio de su esfera?») and indicates how readily the occasional sonnet is converted into something comical and ridiculous. The sonnet is to be found in *Rimas de Tomé de Burguillos,* ed. J. M. BLECUA (Barcelona: Planeta, 1976), p. 50.

it actually represents and what we might have expected it to mean — encapsulate the antithesis of beauty and violence that is present in much of the sonnet. Aldana unfortunately succumbs to a temptation that commonly arises in the occasional sonnet. He strives too ·hard to exploit the event and the outcome is a series of contrivances. Apart from the forced indignation I referred to above, Aldana over-uses the jealousy motif arising from the contrast of the two suns, the lady (i. e. the poet's sun: «mi día») and the real sun, Apollo («el rubio dios»). The frequent repetitions of «luz» —light of the sun and the lady's eyes— serve to sustain this conceit, but by the first tercet the poet appears to be obsessed by repetition as the imperative form «goza» is twice repeated alongside the thrice-repeated «luz». Such features are symptoms of the poet's intention to inflate his material: to give the subject a rhetorical and emotional significance that is altogether out of proportion and beyond the scope of the occasional sonnet with its reliance on lightness and wit. Aldana's sonnet does not become preposterous, as sometimes happens with the more frivolous Petrarchists, [13] but it becomes ponderous and, indeed, in the case of the over-long twelfth line, metrically deficient, as though the form was unable to bear the unexpected weight of meaning. This is a pity for it detracts from more positive features: the irony in the verb «vencía» applied to the lady's beauty after she has been struck (a reverse of the irony of the term «hielo» applied to the man's hand); and the splendid triple alliteration on *r*, *b*, and *z* in the fourth line («tu*r*bar mi pa*z*, *r*obar su lu*z*»). The poem as a whole is unconvincing: the idea of the lady's beauty is handled in a way that is both highly conventional and extravagant. Like his indignation, the poet's praise does not ring true, even on a purely ludic level.

This same contrast of beauty and force is the subject for the classically structured *soneto* II, a poem whose symmetrical exposition has been described by Rivers: [14]

> Junto a su Venus tierna y bella estaba
> todo orgulloso Marte horrible y fiero,
> cubierto de un templado y fino acero
> que un claro espejo al sol de sí formaba;
> y mientras ella atenta en él notaba
> sangre y furor, con rostro lastimero
> un beso encarecido al gran guerrero
> fijó en la frente y dél todo colgaba.
> Del precioso coral tan blando efeto
> salió que al fiero dios del duro asunto
> hizo olvidar con nuevo ardiente celo.

[13] As with poets such as Tebaldeo (1463-1537) and Serafino (1466-1500). See FORSTER, *The Icy Fire*, pp. 24-26; and JOHN A. SCOTT, «Lyric and Pastoral Poetry: Italy», in *The Continental Renaissance*, pp. 140-41.

[14] *Francisco de Aldana, el Divino Capitán*, pp. 153-55; *Poesías*, p. xxxvi.

¡Oh fuerza estraña, oh gran poder secreto:
que pueda un solo beso en sólo un punto
los dioses aplacar, dar ley al cielo!

(R, 3)

The idea of beauty in itself again interests Aldana less than its confrontation with and, in this case, victory over an apparently more powerful element. This is a major issue in the *Otavas en diversas materias* and the similarities between the sonnet and sections of this work are evident both in theme and presentation, notably in the recourse to myth as a source of analogy. The sonnet under consideration is certainly a more accomplished poem than *soneto* V. The obvious semantico-structural contrasts seen at the start («tierna y bella» — «horrible y fiero») could so easily have been abused but on this occasion Aldana keeps a tight rein on such impulses, and is thus able to devote his attention to matters of visual and narrative interest rather than merely labour an antithesis. He succeeds in breathing life and movement into the scene as witness the splendid description of Mars's armour and the fine realization of the moment when Venus plants a kiss on his brow. The brief instant of tension and uncertainty suggested by the last word of the second quatrain («colgaba») yields to a feeling of serenity reflected in the smooth and sonorous line that immediately follows. The Petrarchist metaphor for Venus's lips («precioso coral») seems entirely appropriate in view of the surprising transformation that they achieve.

Nearly all the poems considered thus far have certain features in common. Their frame of reference — whether serious or witty — is conventionally Petrarchist; they do not reveal depths of emotion and, with the exception of *soneto* VIII, they are straightforward in structure and syntax (the complexity of *soneto* I being more apparent than real). On this basis, and when set alongside other sonnets and longer poems to be considered in the following two chapters, it seems fair to assume that they are early works, unexceptional in theme and unadventurous as regards presentation and style. Indeed, apart from *sonetos* VIII and IX (of which more below) it is likely that the first eleven sonnets in Rivers's edition comprise the earlier period in Aldana's career as love poet and sonneteer.

Of the remaining love sonnets, one, in particular, however, gives the impression of being an earlier work than its position in Rivers's edition might imply. This is the mediocre *soneto* XIX:

«Solías tú, Galatea, tanto quererme,
con un deseo tan vivo y tan ardiente,
que estando un solo punto de mí ausente,
de perdida temías luego perderme.
Agora, ya crüel, no puedes verme.
¿Cuál nueva sinrazón, cuál accidente,
nueva tigre crüel, nueva serpiente,
te hacen contra mí sin defenderme?»

33

Tirsis dijo esto, convertido en río,
y queriendo seguir: «El niño arquero
sabe, mi bien, cuán grave mal sostengo»,
    responde ella llorando: «Ay Tirsis mío,
si más que estos dos ojos no te quiero,
que pierda yo la luz que en ellos tengo!»

(R, 13)

Technically and stylistically the sonnet is deficient. The first line is over-long by a syllable or two (depending on whether «solías» is read as a two- or three-syllable word) and the final rhyme —the one concerning the last line of the tercets— is a weak one («sostengo», «tengo»). The tendency to binary phrase-structures in the quatrains leads to some undistinguished realizations («tan vivo y tan ardiente»), while the periphrastic allusion to Cupid («el niño arquero») has no particular function other than to fill a space. But in two respects this sonnet reveals traits of what we shall eventually define as Aldana's mature style. In the first place, he uses dialogue as a means of expressing the feelings of the male and female protagonists, a device used to telling effect in three or four of his mature sonnets but not employed in this way in the earlier ones. Secondly, the Petrarchist stock-in-trade for a rapid characterization of the disdainful lady and the rejected lover is here incorporated in what appears to be no more than a lovers' tiff: Tirsis complains to Galatea that she no longer loves him as before and she vehemently reassures him that this is not so. But the terms in which this intimate exchange is realized suggest more the rigidly formal relationship of the courtly tradition. The poet's complaint at his mistress's harshness is couched in extreme but standard language: she is cruel with the cruelty of a tiger (in other contexts, often a Hircanian tiger) and the venom of a snake. At the same time, he, like many a conventional lover, bemoans the vagaries of fortune. He is transformed into a river —a condensed metaphor deriving from the conceit of the lover's tears forming a stream.

But while this application of Petrarchist language and imagery for non-Petrarchist situations is not elsewhere apparent among the early sonnets, it is used again in a far more daring, not to say iconoclastic, fashion in one of Aldana's finest love sonnets, *soneto* XVII:

Mil veces digo, entre los brazos puesto
de Galatea, que es más que el sol hermosa;
luego ella, en dulce vista desdeñosa,
me dice, «Tirsis mío, no digas esto.»
    Yo lo quiero jurar, y ella de presto
toda encendida de un color de rosa
con un beso me impide y presurosa
busca atapar mi boca con su gesto.
    Hágole blanda fuerza por soltarme,
y ella me aprieta más y dice luego:
«No lo jures, mi bien, que yo te creo.»

> Con esto de tal fuerza a encadenarme
> viene que Amor, presente al dulce juego,
> hace suplir con obras mi deseo.
>
> (R, 12)

As Tirsis and Galatea embrace, the former compliments the girl on her beauty by means of the cliché, «más que el sol hermosa». Galatea's reaction is subtly conveyed in the phrase «en dulce vista desdeñosa», which suggests an initial pleasure at the remark followed by the suspicion that it is flippant rather than heartfelt. The lover's protestations of sincerity provoke the girl's blushes. This is charmingly realized in the phrase «toda encendida de un color de rosa» where the common Petrarchist comparison of the lady's cheeks to roses is given a novel function. Terms like «desdeñosa» (1. 3) and «encadenarme» (1. 13) which could figure conventionally in a context of unfulfilled love to refer respectively to the *amada's* hostility and the hapless lover's ensnaring by love are likewise suffused with a different resonance in this sonnet. The Petrarchist code thus contributes in a surprising way to the description of an unpetrarchan scene, whose emotional and psychological potential has been finely realized. Here Aldana revives a worn tradition, pouring new wine into the old bottles of courtly-Petrarchist ideology and terminology. The gulf between this poem and the early sonnets is obvious, and it is evidence that we are justified in speaking of separate periods in connection with the love poems, an impression that is confirmed by the sonnets to be considered in the next chapter.

For the moment, however, I turn to poems which could be seen as marking a transition between the two periods. In this matter, too, as with the quasi-autobiographical *soneto* X, we are confronted by a sonnet that seems to invite a literal reading. By so doing, we might imagine that *soneto* VII refers to a change of style or theme. The poet-shepherd bemoans the departure of his beloved from the banks of the Arno to those of the Sebeto — more prosaically, from Florence to Naples. In this sonnet, the poet speaks of a new song, a change presumably provoked by the *amada's* departure:

> Que escuches, nueva Aurora, el nuevo intento
> de mi zampoña rústica y subida
> do no consiente y llega su destino...
>
> (R, 7)

But such a resolution to start a new song is a convention of pastoral verse as is the assumption of a modest pose. [15] In any case, there is little evidence

---

[15] Cf. GARCILASO, *Eclogue* III, ll. 41-44:

> Aplica, pues, un rato los sentidos
> al bajo son de mi zampoña ruda,
> indigna de llegar a tus oídos,
> pues d'ornamento y gracia va desnuda...
>
> (*Ed. cit.,* pp. 194-95)

in this sonnet of any practical realization of such an intention: it clearly belongs with the group that I have categorized as early sonnets. The transition is, I believe, seen in *sonetos* VIII and IX. I have already drawn attention to the former when compared with other, early, sonnets that deal with the idea of the lady's beauty and the lover's suffering, but *soneto* IX represents, even more, a significant advance on the sonnets of the first period. The theme — the perils of love — is one that Aldana hardly ever touches upon, though it is common enough in other Golden Age poets, notably Villamediana.[16] The theme is, in a sense, appropriate for this particular sonnet, as it is certainly a more ambitious and sophisticated poem than anything seen thus far:

> ¿Cuál nunca osó mortal tan alto el vuelo
> subir, o quien venció más su destino,
> mi clara y nueva luz, mi sol divino,
> que das y aumentas nuevo rayo al cielo,
>  cuanto el que pudo en este bajo suelo,
> oh estrella amiga, oh hado peregrino,
> los ojos contemplar que de contino
> engendran paz, quietud, guerra y recelo?
>  Bien lo sé yo, que Amor, viéndome puesto
> do no sube a mirar con mucha parte
> olmo, pino, ciprés, ni helado monte,
>  de sus ligeras alas dióme presto
> dos plumas y me dijo: «Amigo, ¡guarte
> del mal suceso de Ícaro o Faetonte!»
>
> (R, 7)

The opening rhetorical question spans both quatrains and contains within the one sentence a whole range of emotional meaning. The opening line is positively menacing: the muted *staccato* articulation spills over in an *enjambement* that highlights the key idea of the sonnet — «subir». By a judicious use of hyperbaton the poet also locates another key word, «mortal», at the centre of the first line, thus enabling it to contain the main metrical stress. Offsetting this «minor-key» resonance is the luminous apostrophe in the third and fourth lines. Indeed, such is the contrast, both of mood and rhythm, that one overlooks the conventional nature of the address to the lady. A notable feature of the second quatrain, and one without parallel in the sonnets studied thus far, is the ability or willingness to modify an established phrase-structure: the pattern of noun plus epithet present in lines five and six is replaced in the eighth by an enumeration of nouns alone. The last line of the second quatrain, though applied to the eyes of the *amada*,

---

[16] ALDANA hints at the idea of the lover's rashness in the opening section of his *Fábula de Faetonte*, although it is not developed into a key issue of this poem. I refer to this in Chapter 4, p. 56. The theme of love's dangers is seen in Villamediana in his predilection for the myth of Icarus in a number of his love sonnets. Like ALDANA, VILLAMEDIANA also composed a long poem on the fable of Phaeton. See his *Obras*, ed. J. M. ROZAS (Madrid: Castalia, 1969), pp. 78-80; 103; 105; 203-66.

also sums up the varying emotional responses of the lover as he embarks on his quest, though this same variety has been generated expressively in the preceding lines: what is semantically explicit in the eighth line has been metrically, syntactically and structurally reflected previously. The tercets are no less subtle. The four-fold division of line eight is repeated in the last line of the first tercet, though the preceding two lines (ll. 9-10), with a fair sprinkling of monosyllabic words, provide a rhythmic contrast to the measured tread of the second quatrain. Impressive too is the effect of dramatization in the final tercet. The recourse to *enjambement* and direct speech (the latter to be a conspicuous feature of the mature sonnets) underlines the feeling of warning mingled with a challenge, while the brevity and abruptness of the concluding mythological allusions (so different to their ponderous use in *soneto* I) lend a threatening and ominous air to the sonnet's close, thus creating a mood that parallels the one found in the opening two lines.

The factor that leads me to the view that this sonnet belongs to the transition period rather than the mature one is its subject-matter; none of the remaining, later-period sonnets concern themselves with the standard Petrarchist amatory situation. Admittedly in terms of style and versification, *soneto* IX is one of Aldana's most assured poems, but its very sophistication of structure and syntax may be another reason for not ascribing it to the second or later period, for in many of these poems there is less concern with the formal aspects and structural potentialities of the sonnet and more with an exploration of its possibilities as a vehicle for scene-creation, characterization and dialogue. There may, indeed, be some justification for dating *sonetos* VIII and IX around 1566-68 in view of their tendency to hyperbaton and syntactical complexity. As was shown in the previous chapter, such features are characteristic of some longer poems of this period, especially the verse epistles. This would consequently imply that *sonetos* I-VII, X, XI and XIX are pre-1566 and certainly there is nothing in these poems to make one argue for a later date. The clearly distinct second group would then belong to a period of a few years following 1568. Perhaps Aldana's predilection for dialogue in the sonnets of this period is a result of his experience with an informal and pseudo-colloquial manner in the verse epistles of the late 1560s. What, I believe, is highly unlikely is that any of the thematically original and sometimes stylistically innovative poems of the second group could precede any of those that I have defined as belonging to an early period. These first love poems of Aldana may have aroused the admiration of his contemporaries; even by the early 1560s Aldana had been praised for his verse. But these poems would not have secured him a place higher than that of his admirers in the judgement of posterity. Were his reputation to have rested on the compositions considered in this chapter he would now be regarded as a minor and erratic talent, occasionally inspired but more frequently mediocre. What makes Aldana a major love poet are the poems of transition and, more especially, those that belong to the later period.

# 3

## LOVE POETRY (2) — THE MATURE POEMS:
## FULFILMENT AND LOSS

In the preceding chapter I suggested that the love poetry of Aldana was at first sight remarkable for its emphasis on the theme of love fulfilled and that it was likely that the sonnets that deal with this subject belong to a later period than those that are concerned with a more conventional view of love and courtship. What I would be reluctant to do is to reduce or to relate this poetic development to a biographical level. Little, if anything, is known of Aldana's emotional life and to attempt to fill the void by too literal a reading of the sonnets, and, worse, to attempt a chronology of possible relationships on that basis would be no more than futile guesswork. Even if the name Galatea, that is so favoured in Aldana's most passionate poetry, were to refer to a Florentine lady (perhaps the same one whose departure from Florence is lamented in *soneto* VII), this would not necessarily imply that the composition of the poems was contemporaneous with the events or experiences that might be extrapolated from them. In fact one could just as safely deduce that the poems that obey a Petrarchan ethos were written at the same time as a possible or probable liaison with «Galatea» or «Filis-Galatea»; indeed such a deduction on artistic grounds seems if anything more plausible. To discard or relegate the conventional and launch into what was a relatively novel approach would involve greater technical and expressive problems than encountered hitherto. We have already seen from *soneto* XVII Aldana's success in such a venture: his imaginative adaptation of the Petrarchan code for an unconventional function. There is every reason to suppose that Aldana relished and needed the challenge offered by a different amatory emphasis and perspective.

Yet there may be some evidence too of a more radical disillusionment with the rigidity and formality of the courtly approach. This is implicit in the poetic quality of the two groups of sonnets and in the fact that the conventional themes are only a source of inspiration when there is a possibility of playful or even frivolous realization, as witness the relative success of *sonetos* V and VIII. This disillusionment is, however, explicit in one poem, in what Rivers has labelled *Copla* II (R, 141), a poem made up of four *quintillas.* In this composition, the poet refers to two approaches to love. One is based on non-attainment and adoration from a distance:

> Sin tantas filosofías,
> hay dos linajes de amor,
> uno amigo de porfías
> que entretiene al servidor                    5
> en necias hipocresías...

The other, that he favours, involves the gratification of his desires:

> es el otro más humano,
> más blando y de más holgura,
> y da la fruta madura
> de invierno como verano,
> y es el que siempre más dura.                  10

In the final *quintilla,* the two attitudes are more directly contrasted:

> Tú por gran descanso tienes
> tu diosa siempre adorar,
> mas por más que me condenes,
> si ocasión se viene a dar,
> yo gustaré de más bienes.                      20

Admittedly this is but a single poem and for that reason it would be rash to give it undue prominence. Nonetheless, the scathing tone of the first stanza and the note of defiant self-justification in the last («por más que me condenes») perhaps indicate an impatience with courtly love, if not as a part of life then at least as a poetic ideology. As we read the later sonnets, however, it becomes evident that the emotional experiences that arise from a view of love fulfilled are far more complex than those suggested by the assertion of the pleasures of carnal love («la fruta madura»; «yo gustaré de más bienes») in the *Copla.*

I begin with *soneto* XII, a poem that has aroused a certain curiosity among literary historians and anthology compilers. The reasons for this are immediately obvious. Both the subject-matter and the graphic nature of the description are such as to make it a highly unusual poem for its period:

> «¿Cuál es la causa, mi Damón, que estando
> en la lucha de amor juntos trabados
> con lenguas, brazos, pies y encadenados
> cual vid que entre el jazmín se va enredando
> y que el vital aliento ambos tomando
> en nuestros labios, de chupar cansados,
> en medio a tanto bien somos forzados
> llorar y suspirar de cuando en cuando?»

«Amor, mi Filis bella, que allá dentro
nuestras almas juntó, quiere en su fragua
los cuerpos ajuntar también tan fuerte
    que no pudiendo, como esponja el agua
pasar del alma al dulce amado centro,
llora el velo mortal su avara suerte.»

(R, 9)

This sonnet has provoked controversy as well as passing interest. For Rivers, the poem is «único por su tema y el realismo de su lenguaje»; indeed he finds the diction «chocante»: «¿en qué otro soneto amoroso del siglo XVI se encontrarán las palabras 'lenguas, braços y pies', ni mucho menos 'chupar'?».[1] He contends that it is a sensual poem in which amatory theory —Neoplatonism specifically— has been bypassed: «Lo que hizo Aldana en este soneto fue sencillamente pasar por alto este aspecto trascendental, y por ende supremo, del amor neoplatónico» (p. 44). This interpretation is contested by Otis H. Green in his review of Rivers' study. He is unconvinced by the claim for Aldana's originality of diction and cites occurrences of the same words in other poems of the period.[2] Moreover he questions Rivers' assertion regarding the poem's lack of philosophical intent. He compares it with the religious sonnet *Al cielo* (*soneto* XXXVII) and is of the opinion that the two poems form «the obverse and reverse of a single thought. And that thought is Platonic» (p. 122). He defines *soneto* XII as «a demonstration —versified from a pasage in León Hebreo— that sensual love cannot give satisfaction: *Post coitum omne animal triste*» (p. 122).

What this debate overlooks too readily, in my opinion, is the emotional effect of the poem *qua* poem. Both Rivers, by his extrapolation of individual words, and Green, with his reduction of the poem's message to the versifying of a snippet of amatory philosophy, pay insufficient attention to the intrinsic poetic factors. Even Ruiz Silva dedicates comparatively little space to an analysis of the sonnet, preferring instead to give a detailed account of the Rivers-Green debate.[3]

The sonnet owes its memorable intensity to several factors rather than to a single philosophical outlook or the lack of one. That its concern is to demonstrate the inadequacy of human love is obvious, and this melancholy conclusion is structurally pinpointed by the strategic positioning of the verb «llora(r)» at the start of the last line of the quatrains and tercets respectively. But the poem's daring and piquancy cannot be explained by idea alone, especially as this idea, according to Green, can be summed up in a Latin

---

[1] *Francisco de Aldana, el Divino Capitán,* p. 156.
[2] «On Francisco de Aldana», pp. 124-28.
[3] *Estudios sobre Francisco de Aldana,* pp. 97-101. An illuminating analysis of this sonnet is to be found in ARTHUR TERRY, «Thought and Feeling in Three Golden Age Sonnets», *Bulletin of Hispanic Studies,* 59 (1982), 237-46 (at pp. 239-40).

tag. A remarkable feature of the sonnet is the contrast between situation and articulation, embodied in the dialogue. For the intimacy of the scene and relationship is evoked in the context of a long and formally-phrased question. In particular, the opening interrogation — «¿Cuál es la causa?» rather than what might have seemed a more appropriately colloquial «¿por qué?» — provides an expectation of theorizing or debate, probably in abstract rather than concrete terms and certainly not in the explicit, sexual rationalization that we have here. But there is another twist or surprise later in the poem. No sooner have we digested the vivid depiction of the quatrains with their heady, almost celebratory, air than we are confronted with a paradox: why should such an ecstatic experiencing of carnal love result in anguish? The answer, expressed in Damón's reply, that sensual love cannot fully satisfy is thus only a *part* of the experience communicated in the sonnet. For what Aldana has done is to have conveyed a whole process of experience, reaction and rationalization rather than merely to embellish a philosophical commonplace. Moreover he reflects in the very development and shape of the sonnet the notions of false expectation, excitement and eventual disillusionment. It generates an emotional dynamism and restlessness by its internal poetic value and not by the truth of the theory or doctrine to which it alludes. The theory —the commonplace even— is located in a context of experienced reality of which it is but an aspect or an outcome, not the trigger or germ. The conclusion is not apprehended by deduction or reasoning; it is learnt because it has been painfully experienced by the protagonists. The impression is that of a truth that has been suddenly encountered.

Partly because of this unwillingness to confront the poetic merits of the sonnet and thus to appreciate its full emotional significance, commentators have been less than successful in relating it to other poems by Aldana. The misrepresentation is two-fold. On the one hand, the graphic description of the sexual act and the directness of the language are by no means as unusual as Rivers has implied. Such features are present in other poems too. Consider, for instance, the passage from the *Otavas en diversas materias* in which Jupiter, disguised as a shower of gold, makes love to Danae:

> Quando con nuuezilla reluziente       505
> Del sesto Cielo aca baxò la Estrella:
> En lluuia de Oro liquida, y corriente
> Se està de Acrisio la Real Donzella,
> La qual viendo caer tan blandamente
> El granizo gentil que da sobre ella,       510
> Las faldas alça, y mientras hinche el seno
> Halla de vn nuevo hijo el vientre lleno.

(OC, II, 157)

41

In the highly erotic *Medoro y Angélica,* the poet relates how Cupid rapturously gazes on the splendours of Angélica's naked body. The listing of the girl's physical attributes has nothing of a Petrarchan decorum about it:

> La sábana después quïetamente
> levanta al parecer no bien siguro,                    50
> y como espejo el cuerpo ve luciente,
> el muslo cual aborio limpio y puro;
> contempla de los pies hasta la frente
> las caderas de mármol liso y duro,
> las partes donde Amor el cetro tiene,                 55
> y allí con ojos muertos se detiene.
>
> (R, 77)

On the other hand, there has been a tendency to see the theme and mood of *soneto* XII as representative of Aldana's love poetry or at least of those poems in which he refers to fulfilment. This is, I believe, quite mistaken. My observations in the previous chapter concerning the variety of Aldana's amatory verse and his tendency not to repeat himself are borne out no less in a number of poems where he deals with the idea of love fulfilled. In the two longer poems to which I have just referred, we encounter a view that is distinctively different to and more positive than that found in *soneto* XII. In the *Otavas en diversas materias,* the poet, by means of a number of *exempla,* demonstrates the necessity and inevitability of the reproductive urge, including, as a culminating point, the observation that:

> Hasta en el Angel ay tanta luxuria
> De pegarse al Autor, por quien se informa...          524
>
> (OC, II, 158)

Rivers sees these lines as a synthesis of sensuality and Christianity;[4] in fact, the governing theory for the poem's message is again Neoplatonic. But while the guiding hand in *soneto* XII is León Hebreo, in the *Otavas en diversas materias* it is Plato and Ficino, specifically the latter's observations on Diotima's exposition of the purpose and benefits of love at the start of Chapter 11 of this section of his *Commentary on Plato's Symposium.*[5] Another passage from this section is the probable inspiration for the attitude towards carnal love in *Medoro y Angélica.* In this poem, the intention is to communicate the beauty and naturalness of sexual love, and the opening *octava*

---

[4] *Poesías,* p. xvi.
[5] «We all desire to have goods, and not only to have them but to have them eternally. The single goods or mortals change and fade and they would all quickly disappear if new ones were not continuously made in place of those which leave. Therefore, so that goods may somehow endure for us forever, we desire to recreate those which pass away. That re-creation is effected by generation. Hence has been born in everyone the instinct for generation.» *Ed. cit.,* pp. 202-03.

and closing line clearly relate this view to the notion of procreative love as a boon, as a God-given gift. The poem opens thus:

> Gracia particular que el alto cielo
> quiso otorgar al bajo mundo en suerte
> es la de dos amantes que en el suelo
> viven con fuego igual, con igual muerte:
> verse la llama helar, arder el hielo,          5
> un pecho quebrantar de mármol fuerte
> y que tan alto ser de amor reciba
> que uno viva por él y el otro viva.
>
> (R, 75)

At the end, the poet refers to «la paz (i. e., fulfilment in love) que tanto al Cielo agrada» (R, 78). Compare the following lines from Ficino's *Commentary:*

> But since generation, by continuation, renders mortal things like divine, it is certainly a divine gift. Because divine things are beautiful, they are opposite to ugly things, and are similar to and consonant with beautiful things. Therefore, generation, which is a divine function, is carried out exactly and easily in that which is beautiful, and the contrary in the opposite. Wherefore the impulse for generation seeks beautiful things and shuns the opposite (p. 203).

The idea of beauty mentioned here is also given prominence in the poem, in Aldana's idealized description of the two lovers.

Different again is *soneto* XVII — a poem erroneously considered as a companion-piece to *soneto* XII («¿Cuál es la causa, mi Damón?»): [6]

> Mil veces digo, entre los brazos puesto
> de Galatea, que es más que el sol hermosa;
> luego ella, en dulce vista desdeñosa,
> me dice, «Tirsis mío, no digas esto.»
> Yo lo quiero jurar, y ella de presto
> toda encendida de un color de rosa
> con un beso me impide y presurosa
> busca atapar mi boca con su gesto.
> Hágole blanda fuerza por soltarme,
> y ella me aprieta más y dice luego:
> «No lo jures, mi bien, que yo te creo.»
> Con esto de tal fuerza a encadenarme
> viene que Amor, presente al dulce juego,
> hace suplir con obras mi deseo.
>
> (R, 12)

Although the scene and subject bear a superficial resemblance to *soneto* XII, its theme and mood are radically distinct. In *soneto* XII, the euphoria yields

---

[6] See JUAN FERRATÉ, «Siete sonetos de Francisco de Aldana», in *Teoría del poema (ensayos)* (Barcelona: Seix Barral, 1957), pp. 69-80 (at p. 79).

to pessimism; here the poet's aim is to communicate the playfulness and ultimately the overwhelming nature of sexual instinct. Whereas in *soneto* XII, the poet bemoaned the deficiencies of carnal love, here he celebrates its power. As in *soneto* XII, dialogue is employed, the interlocutors being again the lover and his mistress. The exchanges in *soneto* XVII are spare and colloquial, however, contrasting sharply with the carefully structured and rhetorically flavoured utterances in the other poem. As I suggested in the previous chapter, *soneto* XVII is remarkable for its fine characterization of the *amada,* simultaneously aroused and embarrassed.[7] In *soneto* XII, Aldana refers to «la lucha de amor»; in the other sonnet, it is to a «dulce juego». While in the former he conveys the experience of a bitter fact suddenly apprehended, in the latter, he suggests that the scene and the playful exchanges are almost part of the lovers' habitual love-play, hence «mil veces digo». It goes without saying, then, that *soneto* XVII is entirely devoid of amatory philosophy; the nearest it comes to having a point or message is in the final tercet with its description of the overpowering erotic urge. This is only a part of the story of *soneto* XII.

The two sonnets which I have discussed in this chapter constitute contrasting views of fulfilled love, but both, in their differing ways, represent unconventional attitudes. The theme of fulfilled love, nonetheless, encounters one conventional vehicle, at least, in Aldana's poetry, in the shape of *soneto* XVI, which describes a dream recounted by the poet-speaker to his companion:

> Galanio, tú sabrás que esotro día,
> bien lejos de la choza y del ganado,
> en pacífico sueño transportado
> quedé junto a una haya alta y sombría
>     cuando (¿quién tal pensó?) Flerida mía,
> traída allí de amigo y cortés hado,
> llegóse y un abrazo enamorado
> me dió, cual otro agora tomaría.
>     No desperté, que el respirado aliento
> della en mi boca entró süave y puro
> y allá en el alma dió del caso aviso,
>     la cual, sin su corpóreo impedimento,
> por aquel paso en que me vi te juro
> que el bien casi sintió del Paraíso.

(R, 12)

Such poems in which the lover enjoys his mistress' favours in a dream formed an important part of the courtly-Petrarchist tradition. They constituted a safety-valve for the frustrated and decorous lover.[8] Even here, though,

---

[7] We find a similar portrayal of Angélica in *Medoro y Angélica.* See WALTERS, «On the Text, Source and Significance of Aldana's *Medoro y Angélica*», p. 25.
[8] See FORSTER, *The Icy Fire,* p. 12.

Aldana leaves his individual stamp. The opening line has a casual air, appropriate for the tone of one confiding in a friend. The following lines seem to have a symbolic significance. The «choza» and the «ganado» are clearly related to the shepherd's life but in the dream-vision of the sonnet they have been left far behind. What is not altogether certain is whether it is through the function of the dream that the poet-shepherd has been removed or whether he had fallen asleep and dreamt after wandering off to a distant place. In either case, the point seems to be that momentarily, or for the duration of the dream, the pastoral reality —probably indicative of unrequited love— has been forgotten and that the poet has been transported into a world that is mysterious when compared with the homely «choza». The scene comprises an imposing beech-tree that casts its shadow over the poet. The atmosphere created by the single image brings to mind the magical, primitive world of the traditional popular lyric. The sleeping shepherd dreams that his beloved embraces and kisses him. At this point in the sonnet (ll. 8-9) the poet seems to be preparing to exploit the contrast between the pleasure obtained from the dream and the harshness of reality. Such a process is often found in poems of this type, for example Quevedo's sonnet to Floralba and sonnets by Pedro de Tablares and Luis Martín de la Plaza on which the Quevedo poem may be modelled. [9] A common feature of the «dream» sonnet is the tendency to a graphic description of the imagined pleasure or, at least, to a more direct mode of reference than is customary. But Aldana does not adopt this method here. This is especially surprising in view of his readiness to write about sexual love in clear, unambiguous terms elsewhere, but it provides more evidence of his independent spirit. Instead of steering the poem towards sexual explicitness Aldana unexpectedly focusses on the spiritual significance of the kiss, developing it in a Neoplatonic fashion reminiscent of a passage from Luis de León's commentary on the *Song of Solomon*. [10] The prominence given to the idea of the kiss in the tercets may well suggest that the epithet «pacífico» in the third line might be doubly significant: not only the primary meaning of «peaceful» but also one related to the use of the word «paz» as «kiss», a usage deriving from the Mass. Supporting this interpretation is a parallel case near the end of *Medoro y Angélica* where the poet puns repeatedly on the word «paz». There is, finally, another feature of note that adds to the complex register of this sonnet. This occurs in the last line where the poet uses the terms «bien» and «Paraíso» to refer to his dream. Such terminology is commonly found in *cancionero* and Golden Age poetry, especially the former. [11] «Bien» has a multitude of meanings depending on the

---

[9] See FRANCISCO DE QUEVEDO, *Poesía varia*, ed. J. O. CROSBY (Madrid: Cátedra, 1981), pp. 223-24.

[10] As pointed out by RUIZ SILVA, *Estudios sobre Francisco de Aldana*, p. 105.

[11] See KEITH WHINNOM, *La poesía amatoria de la época de los Reyes Católicos* (Durham: University of Durham, 1981), pp. 23; 41.

context, one of which is as a euphemism for sexual fulfilment. «Paraíso» belongs to the semantic field that relies on blasphemy for its effect. Compare for instance the use of the term «cielo» in these lines from a Quevedo *romance* that also alludes to fulfilment in a dream:

> Dime una hartazga de cielo
> en tan altas maravillas,
> y aun dentro de tus dos ojos
> te quise forzar las niñas. [12]

Thus the last line of Aldana's sonnet falls into the category of euphemistic description of erotic activity. This represents another shift in the expressive register of the poem. Graphic description («un abrazo enamorado») is followed by a more spiritual rationalization and this, in turn, by an indirect mode of allusion to physical love. Such a complexity is appropriate for one, confusedly perhaps, recalling the details and circumstances of a dream.

Another subject commonly encountered in Golden Age poetry concerns the poet's endeavours to renounce love —an effort that normally ends in failure. He will think longingly of his past freedom but the power of love or the beloved herself tends to overcome any good intentions. Instances of such poems are to be found in the work of Herrera, Bartolomé Leonardo de Argensola and Quevedo, but the following sonnet by Aldana is reminiscent most of all of one by Lope to Lucinda: [13]

> Juro, Escobar, por aquel lazo eterno,
> nudo de amor, que entre los dos ha dado
> tras discreta elección fuerza de hado,
> en cuya luz la vuestra amo y discierno,
>     que ya que (ya del amoroso infierno
> el fugitivo pie libre he sacado,
> y en puerto de salud llevó el cuidado
> áspero temporal de helado invierno),
>     hecha su redención, vuelve a su gloria
> el alma, adonde por oficio tiene
> perpetüar la risa de su llanto,
>     ¡muera Filis malvada en mi memoria!
> Mas, ay triste de mi, ¿de dónde viene
> nombre tan duro enternecerme tanto?

(R, 10)

Many such sonnets achieve their effect by postponing to the very end the realization that love is too strong a force to overcome and this is the case here. The surprise is enhanced, moreover, by the vehemence of the twelfth line with its alliteration of *m* and by the way in which the poet seems to

---

[12] *Ed. cit.*, p. 485.
[13] These poems are discussed by WALTERS, *Francisco de Quevedo, Love Poet*, pp. 61-69. Lope's sonnet begins «Ya vengo con el voto y la cadena».

conjure up a moment of silent reflection on the very name of the beloved after his exclamation. The sonnet is notable for the extravagance of its figurative language, particularly in the case of the second quatrain where the effect is at first sight seemingly kaleidoscopic: images of the hell of love, a faltering step, a safe haven, a storm and an icy winter succeed each other rapidly, though on closer examination the progression is clear enough. The idea of the lover's hazardous progress and journeying present in the «pie fugitivo» image is continued by the notion of a perilous sea-crossing as seen in the images that refer to the safe harbour and to adverse weather-conditions. The quatrain opens with an appropriately cacophonous phrase — «que ya (que ya...)» — which serves perhaps as a phonetic anticipation of the idea of danger.

The most interesting feature of the sonnet resides, I feel, in the contrast of friendship and love. Ruiz Silva notes how the poem is «a la vez amoroso y de amistad» but claims that the two ideas are treated separately: friendship in the first quatrain and love over the remainder of the sonnet. [14] But Aldana's description of the nature of his bond of friendship with Escobar is couched in such a way as to suggest that a constant comparison of the two kinds of relationship is being entertained. The full extent of the contrast becomes apparent in the course of the second quatrain as the terms used to refer to friendship in the first quatrain encounter antitheses. The poet's relationship with Escobar (whose identity is not known) is seen in terms of permanence and security: «aquel lazo eterno, / nudo de amor»; indeed such a phrase hints at marital fidelity. In fact the poet reserves for his friend a kind of tribute that is normally paid to the beloved when he informs him that «la vuestra [luz] amo y discierno». [15] But when the poet speaks of his relationship with Filis, he presents a radically different picture. It is fraught with menace and unhappiness, hence the «amoroso infierno», and constitutes a condition from which the poet must flee («fugitivo pie»).

As with so many of Aldana's poems there are lines that are not easy to interpret. Such is the case with the phrase «perpetüar la risa de su llanto». Ruiz Silva's suggestion that it refers to the mixed feelings of the poet as he renounces love or at least envisages its renunciation is a sensible one particularly in the light of the last two lines. [16] Of interest too is the third line with its apparent contradiction: the friendship arose from a discerning choice but is sustained by fate. Of this Ruiz Silva writes: «Combina, pues, Aldana el sentido fatalista con el libre albedrío, síntesis realmente original e innovadora adaptada al tema poético de la amistad» (p. 103). But this does not altogether explain why Aldana should refer to the relationship in the way he does. A possible interpretation resides again in the contrast

[14] *Estudios sobre Francisco de Aldana,* p. 102.
[15] «Luz» is the pseudonym for the beloved favoured by Herrera in his love poetry.
[16] *Estudios sobre Francisco de Aldana,* p. 102.

with the amatory aspect. The poet's love for Filis, unlike his friendship with Escobar, presumably arose not from «discreta elección» but from the fateful power of love conquering his free-will. Disillusioned with love, the poet then resolves to exercise his will or discretion and break its hold over him. Ultimately, though, as the sound of the beloved's name rings in his ears (or his imagination, his inner ear) the inexorable «fuerza de hado» of love reasserts itself. The neatness and difficulty of such a poem with its constant comparison and pointing anticipate the manner, if not precisely the methods, of the *conceptista* poets a generation later.

The subject of friendship figures too in *soneto* XV, one of several poems concerned with absence or impending absence. The poet speaks on behalf of himself and his companion, Frónimo, as they lament their separation from their respective mistresses:

> ¿Quién podrá sin un ¡ay! del alma enviado,
> sin lágrimas echar de ciento en ciento,
> sin tanto sospirar que pueda el viento
> las ondas contrastar del mar airado,
>     quien podrá, digo, ¡ay miserable hado!,
> sin dar de sí tan alto sentimiento,
> las dudas declarar de aquel tormento
> que oprimir nuestras almas no ha dudado?
>     Juntos llorar, mi Frónimo, el ausencia
> de mi sol y tu luz ya nos conviene
> más que alma de infernal peso afligida,
>     que si consiste en sola la presencia
> nuestro vivir de quien sin él nos tiene
> ausente, ¿quién sabrá qué cosa es vida?
>
> (R, 11)

A striking feature of this sonnet is its intensity, a trait that can be well appreciated if it is compared with *soneto* VI («Por vuestros ojos juro, Elisa mía») (R, 6). This earlier poem also deals with the absence of the beloved and its consequences upon the poet-shepherd but though it is a competent poem in the standard pastoral vein, it pales into insignificance beside *soneto* XV. This poem is one of the most rhetorical of Aldana's love sonnets. The quatrains, in particular, are carefully composed so as to provide an impression of sonority and pathos. Aldana is sometimes accused, rightly, of obscurity and a lack of polish, but conversely not enough credit is given to him for his technical mastery. The use of anaphora in the sonnet («¿quién?»; «sin») lends a measured dignity to the lament and counter-balances such tellingly shrill effects as the strategic positioning of the exclamation (¡ay!) on or near the main stress (sixth syllable) of the first line of both quatrains; the sustained alliteration of *d* in the second quatrain; and the stutter of the fifth line whose tripartite division enhances the violent hyperbaton in the second quatrain («¿quién podrá declarar las dudas?»). Indeed the sonnet makes greater use of hyperbaton than any other of the sonnets with the possible exception of *soneto* IX. The most striking instance is to be found in the second tercet which should be read as: «que si nuestro vivir consiste en la sola presencia de quien ausente nos tiene sin él (i. e., 'nuestro vivir').» This clause, sprawling over the greater part of the tercet and including a strong *enjambement* («tiene/ausente»), leads to a breathless, almost exhausted, pause after «ausente». The final, brief question that encapsulates the poet's dejection and bewilderment lends the sonnet a stark and simple conclusion —a register markedly different to that encountered in the ponderous, even majestic, quatrains.

The subject of the parting of lovers, no less, inspires Aldana to passionate utterance. In his *soneto* XIII the beloved reproaches her departing lover. The poem thus follows the tradition of the *alba* — a song of parting at dawn — but it is conceived and expressed in a surprisingly vehement fashion:

> De sus hermosos ojos dulcemente
> un tierno llanto Filis despedía
> que por el rostro amado parecía
> claro y precioso aljófar trasparente;
>     en brazos de Damón, con baja frente,
> triste, rendida, muerta, helada y fría,
> estas palabras breves le decía,
> creciendo a su llorar nueva corriente:
>     «¡Oh pecho duro, oh alma dura y llena
> de mil durezas! ¿Dónde vas huyendo?
> ¿Dó vas con ala tan ligera y presta?»
>     Y él, soltando de llanto amarga vena,
> della las dulces lágrimas bebiendo,
> besóla, y sólo un ¡ay! fue su respuesta.

(R, 10)

The diction employed in the first quatrain is consistent with the plangent and gentle tone of pastoral. The opening is rounded off by a metaphor for tears («aljófar») that is for Aldana unusually lush. But as so often the reader is to be surprised, for the second quatrain does not continue in the same melancholy vein. In the first place, the poet describes the lovers' farewell in terms of physical intimacy («en brazos de Damón»), and this is followed by an emphatic evocation of the girl's sadness and despair. For this he employs no fewer than five epithets, but apart from the sheer number, the very nature of the three central adjectives («rendida, muerta, helada») conveys the sense of emotional upheaval in very physical terms. Again it is notable how common Petrarchist terminology is given an uncommon significance. «Helada» and «fría» would normally be words that described the disdainful unapproachable lady; here, they are used in a context that depicts the very opposite of this. The concentration on the physical aspect is underlined by the description of the lover kissing his mistress' tears by means

49

of the vivid verb «bebiendo». Indeed, taken overall, the sonnet outlines the pain of the impending separation in terms that could be taken to imply post-coital disenchantment; words like «rendida» and «muerta» certainly provide this impression. The sense of loss and exhaustion, the *amada*'s «breves palabras» and then the mere sigh «¡ay!» (as with *soneto* XV at a climactic point in the line; in the case of the present sonnet, the last line) all serve to conjure up an experience of physical malaise and deprivation. The words that Aldana puts into the girl's mouth suggest an effort at verisimilitude in the lack of eloquence, hence the repetition: «duro», «dura», «durezas». This intention is somewhat marred, however, by the inappropriate use of a metaphor: «ala tan ligera y presta.»

Aldana's predilection for dialogue and for an attempt at recapturing natural speech is taken to an extreme in his *soneto* XVIII, another poem concerned with the lover's departure from his beloved:

> «¿Ya te vas, Tirsis?» «Ya me voy, luz mía.»
> «¡Ay muerte!» «¡Ay Galatea, qué mortal ida!»
> «Tirsis, mi bien, ¿dó vas?» «Do la partida
> halle el último fin de mi alegría.»
> «¿Luego en saliendo el sol?» «Saliendo el día.»
> «¿Te vas sin dilatar?» «Me voy sin vida.»
> «¡Ay Tirsis mío!» «¡Ay gloria mía perdida!»
> «¡Mi Tirsis!» «¡Galatea, mi estrella y guía!»
> «¿Quién tal podrá creer?» «No hay quien tal crea.»
> «¡Oh muerte!» «Acabaré yo mis enojos.»
> «¡Ay grave mal!» «¡Ay mal grave y profundo!»
> «Tirsis, adiós.» «Adiós, mi Galatea.»
> «¡Tirsis, adiós!» «Adiós, luz de mis ojos.»
> «¡Oh lástima!» «¡Oh piedad, sola en el mundo!»

> (R, 13)

Although this is an eye-catching poem, it does not seem to me as powerful an utterance as the previous sonnet. The sheer number of the exchanges does not of itself create greater tension or drama, and in this I differ from Ruiz Silva who interprets the sonnet in terms of «una secuencia teatral aislada». [17] If such a dialogue were to be acted out the effect would hardly be theatrically convincing; indeed it might verge on the ridiculous. As a poem, the multiple exchanges between the protagonists do not disguise a certain poverty of idea. A number of the lines serve merely to mark time and are in the nature of padding, for example, the inappropriately ponderous last phrase of the first quatrain which even Ruiz Silva finds «en exceso vaga y difusa» (p. 108), and the last four lines of the poem where the various repetitions («grave mal», «mal grave», «adiós») suggest more a running out of ideas than emotional intensification. The one idea of note in the poem

[17] *Ibid.*, p. 108.

is the use made of imagery of light. On the one hand, the beloved is described as the poet's light or star («luz mía», «mi estrella y guía», «luz de mis ojos») —a standard Petrarchist-Neoplatonic compliment— but light is seen in a more negative way also as the coming of the new day that marks the lovers' separation, for this sonnet is again in the *alba* tradition. But Aldana does not exploit this contrast as much as its potential allows, certainly not by comparison with the friendship-love opposition in *soneto* XIV. Doubtless the self-imposed formula of two utterances per line for the greater part of the sonnet is a handicap, depriving the poet of the possibility of depth in his shaping of the scene and in his creation of emotional interaction between the protagonists.

Although this is not one of Aldana's most successful poems, it nonetheless shows a refreshing willingness to experiment. Indeed most of his mature sonnets —the poems considered in this chapter— provide evidence of innovation in a number of respects: in subject-matter, amatory outlook and handling of the medium of the sonnet. It is reasonable to assume an evolution in Aldana's conception of the sonnet's potentiality from such classically shaped poems as *soneto*s II, III and XI with their adherence to formal divisions, through the syntactically more adventurous *soneto*s VIII and IX, to the more direct, trenchant and sometimes colloquial utterances of the sonnets considered in this chapter. Aldana does not altogether eschew the rhetorical possibilities of the sonnet as witness *soneto* XV, but it cannot be said that he showed much interest in exploiting the form for a grand or sonorous effect. Instead he seems to have been seeking a variety of register and a flexibility in structural matters that could extend to the acommodation of dialogue and natural speech-patterns. He builds on the achievements of Garcilaso and the first generation of Spanish Petrarchists in a markedly different way to Herrera, his contemporary, and especially to the young Góngora whose love sonnets written in the 1580s have little in common, either thematically or structurally, with Aldana's. [18] There is less reliance on myth and mythological allusion than with other Golden Age poets. Unlike Góngora, Aldana seems to have curbed a trend towards hyperbaton, a feature discernible in the poetry he wrote in the late 1560s though even in this he is no more adventurous than, say, Fray Luis de León. [19] Aldana uses the image or the symbol (though by no means profusely) rather than metaphor or simile in his love sonnets; the simile «como esponja el agua» in *soneto* XII

---

[18] Consider, for example, the emphasis on sophistications of structural detail within an entirely conventional amatory context in such sonnets as: «De pura honestidad templo sagrado», «Tras la bermeja Aurora el Sol dorado», «Raya, dorado Sol, orna y colora», «Suspiros tristes, lágrimas cansadas», «Rey de los otros, río caudaloso», «Ni en este monte, este aire, ni este río», «No destrozada nave en roca dura». *Sonetos completos*, ed. BIRUTÉ CIPLIJAUSKAITÉ, 3rd edn (Madrid: Castalia, 1978), pp. 118-36.

[19] See RAFAEL LAPESA, «El hipérbaton en la poesía de Fray Luis de León», in *Studies in Spanish Literature of the Golden Age Presented to Edward M. Wilson*, ed. R. O. Jones (London: Tamesis Books, 1973), pp. 137-47.

is thus all the more striking for its rarity. Interestingly, in his longer poems, especially the *Carta para Arias Montano,* metaphor and simile are very much to the forefront. Aldana must have felt that such figurative devices would detract from the concision and abruptness that he sought in many of his love sonnets. This, then, constitutes another departure from the practices of earlier Spanish Petrarchists: the extended simile is a fairly common feature in such poets as Hurtado de Mendoza and Cetina —a trait inherited from Boscán and Ausiàs March. [20]

Aldana's chief originality resides thematically in his treatment of the subject of fulfilled love and stylistically in his recourse to dialogue within the sonnet-form. These features are rarely found in sixteenth-century Spanish poetry, and they are also uncommon in the work of Italian poets of the same period. Though direct speech is used, it is seldom employed for dialogue in the way it is in Aldana's mature love sonnets. Thus Rivers' observation that «es difícil relacionar a Aldana con otros poetas, sean españoles o sean italianos» is not one with which to quibble. [21] Nonetheless it seems, in conclusion, a tempting thought that Aldana may have been shown the way by the following sonnet by Benedetto Varchi who was, it should be remembered, his teacher as well as his friend:

> «Cosa al mondo non è che più mi piaccia
> e mi dilette in più soavi tempre,
> caro Tirinto mio, che viver sempre
> e poi morir ne le tue dolci braccia:
>  solo che a te, novello Adon, non spiaccia
> ch'io nel mirarti mi distrugga e stempre,
> e 'l tuo bel guardo, come suol, contempre
> l'ardor che tutta e notte e dì m'agghiaccia.»
>  Queste proprie parole appo la villa
> in cui s'onora il gran divo Ercolano,
> e dove or tutte il ciel sue grazie stilla,
>  cantò, mentre d'amor trema e sfavilla,
> con dolcissime voci in atto umano
> la vaga e felicissima Tesilla. [22]

This is a justly popular anthology piece. Its air of serene and relaxed hedonism epitomizes the grace and charm with which Renaissance poets conjured up the pagan world. But it is neither a vapid nor especially frivolous composition. Indeed in two respects perhaps it points the way forward to Aldana's mature love poems. In the first place, though there is no dialogue

---

[20] For an examination of the imitation by Spanish poets of the generation after Garcilaso of the stylistic traits of Ausiàs March see KATHLEEN MCNERNEY, *The Influence of Ausiàs March on Early Golden Age Castilian Poetry* (Amsterdam: Editions Rodopi B. V., 1982).

[21] *Poesías,* p. xliii.

[22] There is no modern edition of Varchi's poetry. I quote from *Poesia italiana del Cinquecento,* ed. GIULIO FERRONI (Milan: Garzanti, 1978), p. 100.

in the sense of there being an exchange of words, it is clear that there is both a speaker and a specific listener. The words are addressed to Tirinto; what is uncertain is whether this is the poet or whether the poet is merely an onlooker. In either instance, the situation is similar to that found in a number of Aldana's sonnets that treat requited love. It is furthermore significant that Varchi's sonnet also contains a clear reference to fulfilment in the Petrarchist euphemism for the orgasm: «morir ne le tue dolci braccia».[23] Erotically explicit too is the use of the verb «trema» applied to the beloved in the twelfth line: «mentre d'amor trema». The recourse to Petrarchist antitheses in such a context, as seen in the eighth line of the sonnet, is a feature present in the introductory stanza of *Medoro y Angélica:* «viven con fuego igual, con igual muerte: / verse la llama helar, arder el hielo» (R, 75). Admittedly such similarities of approach and realization do not amount to a clear and conscious source nor do they detract from Aldana's individuality. Varchi's sonnet is still some way from both the anguish of Aldana's *soneto* XII and the erotic mischievousness of his *soneto* XVII; it lacks the rough, trenchant quality of Aldana's best love sonnets. But it shows perhaps the perspective within which any statement concerning the Spanish poet's originality should be located. It is from such a poem as Varchi's sonnet that he would have had to depart — this would have been the base camp on his journey of exploration.

[23] See FORSTER, *The Icy Fire,* pp. 19-20.

# 4

# LOVE POETRY (3) — POEMS OF ASPIRATION

For all their variety, the love sonnets of Aldana fall into two clear categories as regards the nature of the amatory experience: unrequited love and sexual fulfilment. Some of his longer poems, however, cannot be as easily defined, and they are far from being mere elaborations of the same issues and experiences that are present in the sonnets. The difference between these and the longer poems is thus not only a matter of form or medium; it concerns idea and approach as well. This difference is evident in the fact that one important aspect of the amatory experience and a common enough subject in Renaissance love poetry is scarcely touched upon in the sonnets, with the exception of *soneto* XI. This revolves around the idea of the lover striving to win the favours or, at least, the recognition of the disdainful lady.

I turn firstly to the poem in *octavas, Medoro y Angélica*. Reference was made to this poem in the previous chapter as an illustration both of a philosophy of love and of graphic eroticism. But the poem is more complex and piquant, even, than this. It is necessary to understand the governing theory or outlook and the boldness of the diction in the context of the situation described in the poem and to be aware that there is a specific addressee, the poet's mistress.[1] The work concludes by contrasting two kinds of amatory reality: the fulfilled love of Medoro and Angélica and the thwarted aspirations of the poet *vis à vis* the lady. The unhappy lover firstly addresses Medoro and reveals his envy at the latter's good fortune in love:

> La paz tomaste, ¡oh venturoso amante!,
> con dulce guerra en brazos de tu amiga;
> y aquella paz, mil veces que es bastante,        75
> nunca me fuera, en paz de mi fatiga:
> triste, no porque paz mi lengua cante
> (paz quieres inmortal, fiera enemiga),
> mas antes, contra amor de celo armada,
> huye la paz, que tanto al Cielo agrada.       80

(R, 78)

[1] See WALTERS, «On the Text, Source and Significance of Aldana's *Medoro y Angélica*», pp. 20, 27.

I have already indicated how this *octava* illustrates Aldana's tendency to lapse into unnecessary obscurity, brought about in this instance by an exaggerated utilization of punning on the word «paz». On the one hand, this implies fulfilment (ll. 1, 3 and 8) and the lovers' kiss (ll. 1 and 3), and, on the other —in the phrase «paz quieres inmortal»— the denial of sexual love, either because it suggests a moralistic opposition to love and an interest on the *amada*'s part in spiritual rather than physical matters,[2] or because it could be understood as relating to the peace of the dead and so be a metaphor for the suffering caused by the lady's refusal.

In this final stanza the contrast between description and narration (the tale of the Ariostan lovers) and situation (the poet and the beloved) is made explicit. But with hindsight it can be seen that much of the poem's content is best understood by being aware of the contrast between the two sets of lovers. Moreover, the poem is shaped and articulated in such a way as to make it seem an attempt to convert the beloved, to persuade her to yield to the poet's demands. At the start, sensual love is seen as being necessary and universal, hence the allusions to Plato and Ficino almost as though they were witnesses of the dignity of love. To drive home the point, the poet paints an alluring picture of the lovers' blissful union in which everything —the intimate setting, the very beauty of the lovers and the serene atmosphere— serves as an enticement. Important too in this connection is the poet's characterization of Angélica. The following lines occur at the point where the sleeping girl has been awakened by Cupid's furtive presence. The god has been rapturously observing the weary lovers, and his role, in all probability, is to represent the envy of the poet-speaker:

> Admirado la mira y dice: «¡Oh cuánto
> debes, Medor, a tu ventura y suerte!»
> Y más quiso decir, pero entre tanto
> razón es ya que Angélica despierte,        60
> la cual con breve y repentino salto,
> viéndose así desnuda y de tal suerte,
> los muslos dobla y lo mejor encubre,
> y por cubrirse más, más se descubre.
>    Confusa, al fin, halló nueva manera,       65
> que a su Medor abraza enternecida
> y con la blanca mano por defuera
> trabaja de quedar toda ceñida...
>
>          (R, 77)

This description brings to mind the charming portrayal of Galatea in *soneto* XVII. Like the girl in the sonnet, Angélica is both coy and passionate. By this portrayal, perhaps, the poet intends to demonstrate to his reluctant mistress that even someone like Angélica, who has yielded to the pleasures of love, has not by so doing lost her girlish innocence and self-respect.

---

[2] This interpretation is suggested by RIVERS, *Poesías*, p. 78n.

The poem thus comprises a sophisticated interplay of intention, description and address. A precedent, albeit a far less ambitious one, is to be found in the *Fábula de Faetonte*. Although he follows the source, Alamanni's *Favola di Phaetonte*, quite closely both as regards general outline and many details, Aldana takes leave from the Italian poem in the dedicatory section of the work.[3] Both poets begin with an invocation to the sun, but whereas Alamanni continues with a dedication to the French king, François I, Aldana addresses an anonymous lady who does not return his love. His first allusion to her consists of an extended and obvious pun on the word «sol» — a characteristic and rather irritating trait:

> Mira a mi sol, ò sol, veras si solo
> Aca como tu alla ser solo puede.
> Mira ondear al viento el sotil oro,
> Y jurar osare con juramento
> Sobre mi sol, ò sol que tambien juras       35
> Por tu misma deidad, que cierto piensas
> Aquellos ser tus rayos, y creydo
> Ternas que ella es el sol, aunque el sol ella
> Iurara sobre si, que eres tu cierto:
> Tanto que en esta diferencia amiga       40
> Seras tu solo alla, y ella aca sola
> Mirados por dos soles, y dos solos.
> (OC, I, 148-49)

Hard on the heels of this association of the *amada* with Apollo comes another identification: Phaeton and his rash, disastrous exploit is related to the poet's own misfortune in love. The passage concludes with a Petrarchist cliché though one that is quite imaginatively applied to the fable. The tears of disappointed love that are the outcome of the poet-lovers's desires are compared to the waters of the Eridanus that receive the charred body of Phaeton.

But this represents the extent of the parallel between the lover and the mythological figure. The analogy is only a fleeting one whereas in *Medoro y Angélica* it forms an integral part of the poem, serving as an instrument of persuasion if not seduction. In both cases, however, the standpoint is rooted in a negative amatory experience: the lover confronted by the coldness and inaccessibility of the *amada*. Such is the situation in two other love poems, the *Otavas en diversa materia* and the *Epístola a una dama cuyo principio falta*. These are principally or ostensibly amatory laments, but they are suffused in various places and in various ways with the hope of alleviation. As a consequence there is more to these poems —especially the *Epístola*— than meets the eye. Beyond the standard Petrarchist complaint there are hints of something deeper and ambiguous.

---

[3] See RUIZ SILVA, *Estudios sobre Francisco de Aldana*, p. 152.

Despite its title, the *Otavas en diversa materia* is recognizably a single poem, unlike the series of *octavas* entitled *Otavas en diversas materias* which, as we have already seen, comprises a long poem and a number of poetic fragments. The title of the former poem may have been suggested by the diffuse nature of the poem, caused mainly by repetition and syntactical obscurity. This suggests an unpolished rather than an unfinished or composite product for the poem clearly has a starting-point and a conclusion. In the first *octava,* the poet expresses his pleasure at the unexpected opportunity of being able to converse with the beloved: «Que por premio especial de mi fatiga / Ordena esta ocasion que os hable y vea» (OC, II, 121); and in the last stanza there is a clear reference to the end of the conversation:

> Todo aquello demas que yo dixera,
> Y escucharlo de vos por carta passe,
> Mi vida a Dios, quedad tan persuadida
> De mi, quanto de vos està mi vida. 264
>
> (OC, II, 133)

One of the weak features of the poem —and something that perhaps gives the impression of a rough draft or of an early work— is the handling of imagery and figurative language. As we have already seen, Aldana is somewhat averse to such devices in his love sonnets and it is possible that he only felt secure in this aspect of technique towards the end of his life, as evidenced by the copious and inspired use of simile in the *Carta para Arias Montano.* Very different are the insipid figures of speech in the *Otavas en diversa materia,* for example, the simile in stanza 12:

> Que mas no dure en vos pesar tan duro
> Huya qual niebla al Sol vana, y ligera... 94
>
> (125)

and the one in stanza 14:

> Huye vn contrario la virtud contraria,
> Como la escuridad la luz viniendo... 110
>
> (126)

In stanza 25, the trite nature of the imagery employed to suggest the idea that misfortune is ephemeral is aggravated by the heavy-handed anaphora:

> No siempre el Ayre està de Nubes lleno,
> No siempre el viento mueue a la Mar guerra,
> No siempre con furor de Rayo, o Trueno 195
> Hiere Ioue inmortal la baxa Tierra:
> Tambien su manto azul, claro, y sereno
> Suele el Cielo mostrar, tambien se encierra
> El viento, el Mar tambien se pone quieto,
> Y Ioue es apazible, y mansueto. 200
>
> (130)

and the following stanza is merely an elaboration of the same idea via a series of commonplace analogies:

> Despues de vn gran viaje el Peregrino
> Buelue al albergue de su vida incierto,
> Corre la Naue el humido camino
> De vn Polo al otro, y goza al fin del puerto:
> A segura salud dudoso vino                               205
> El que poco antes se tenia por muerto,
> Assi terna despues de vn largo vltraje
> Puerto alegre, y salud nuestro viaje.
>
> (130)

These two stanzas are in fact symptomatic of one of the poem's chief deficiencies: it is too long (33 stanzas) for its material. Most of this derives from the following ideas to which the poet frequently returns: the request to the lady for her to provide some alleviation of the lover's suffering; the expectation that she will be willing to grant this, and the feeling that their mutual love will be able to survive and overcome the vicissitudes of fate. But the poem is not entirely shapeless. For example, two sets of *octavas* (stanzas 9 and 10; 16 and 17) occurring almost exactly a quarter and a half of the way through the poem respectively reveal the existence of a particular pattern. In the ninth stanza, the poet believes the beloved's melancholy to be the result of her concern about the power of fate:

> Bien se que esse pesar tan descubierto,                  65
> Esse biuo dolor, que os atormenta,
> Es porque a nuestro amor el hado incierto
> Dificultades mil nos representa...
>
> (124)

This is followed in stanza 10 by the hope, in the form of an exhortation, that love can overcome the fear of what fickle fortune can achieve:

> Pero destruya Amor con dulce zelo,
> Tan amargo pesar, que assi me alcança,
> No pueda esse atreuido desconsuelo                       75
> El fresco Abril dañar de mi esperança...
>
> (124)

Midway through the poem a parallel, though not identical, pattern is to be found. In stanza 16, the poet refers to the lady's unhappiness and once more he makes a supposition. It is a bolder one now. He believes that his mistress is distressed because of the delay to the fulfilment of their love:

> Y si como dezis vuestro tormento
> Nace de la piedad que me teneis,
> Piedad podeis tener del sentimiento,
> Que con vuestro dolor me causareis:
> Si viene porque Amor tarda el contento...               125
>
> (126)

The following lines —consistent with the earlier pattern— declare that fate can be overcome. Whereas in the tenth stanza it was the power of love, now it is both love and the lovers themselves:

> Con las dificultades que sabeis,
> El Amor fuerçe a la fortuna, y pueda
> Nuestra conformidad mas que su rueda.
>
> (126-27)

In the next stanza it is suggested that the beauty of the lady can expel misfortune:

> Mas vos cuya beldad hiere, arde, y prende
> Todo aluedrio, que estè en tormenta, o calma
> Siendo fuerça menor la que pretende
> Llevar de vos la triunfante palma,
> Con solo el reboluer de ojos ayrados          135
> Hazeis temblar las suertes y los hados.
>
> (127)

Both these passages illustrate one of the most interesting features of this flawed composition. They are indicative of a departure from the amatory norms adhered to in other aspects of the work. The poem contains much that is conventional in the context of Spanish Petrarchist poetry. There is the initial satisfaction at a minimal favour, viewed as nothing less than a boon. One could also cite the idea of the blessed suffering and the willing acceptance of the defeat of the faculty of free-will, as in the third *octava*:

> Pues sus querida, y dulce vsurpuadora
> De mi aluedrio, bolued piadosa, y blanda
> Esse rostro gentil, que me enamora
> Hazia estos ojos que le estan mirando:          20
> O sobre todas venturosa el hora,
> Que os di mi libertad, dichoso el quando
> Me llamé vuestro, pues tan dulce, y chara
> Me fue, y sera vuestra hermosa cara.
>
> (122)

There are also several passages of standard eulogy, for example, stanza 22:

> Por esse Oro sutil, nueuo, y luziente,
> Que por mano de Amor se ordena, y mueue,          170
> Por essa de Marfil graciosa frente
> Donde tiene el Abril perpetua nieue?
> Mi Sol os pido, y por la llama ardiente
> Que en mi la luz de vuestros ojos llueue,
> Que abrais a rato mas gracioso, y tierno          175
> El Alma, y gozaran las del Infierno.
>
> (128-29)

Here the Petrarchist description leads to the poet addressing his lady as his sun, an idea found initially in the second stanza («Assi pues vos mi Sol con luz hermosa / Heris mi coraçon tan altamente»).

What is striking about the two sets of stanzas quoted above (stanzas 9 and 10; 16 and 17) is the leap in reasoning made by the poet. In both cases he makes assumptions for which there would appear to be little justification on the basis of the poem's opening stanzas. He believes that the lady's unhappiness (or what he interprets as her unhappiness) derives from a concern (a) that their love might be threatened by misfortune and (b) that fulfilment may be delayed. Indeed it seems that such observations are the product of wishful thinking for such expectations are not confined to the two examples already cited. What is more they increase in boldness. In stanza 5, the poet states that he seems to detect signs that the lady is prepared to acknowledge him, to be more amenable:

> Parece me tambien que en vos ya veo
> Grata, y dulce atencion por colocarme
> Donde a penas llegar puede el desseo...          35
>
> (122)

Further to the assumptions of stanzas 9 and 16, in stanza 20 the poet feels free to refer to «nuestro dessear», in his view no longer a one-sided aspiration but a common emotion. The climax is attained in stanzas 30-32. In the first of these he refers to «la luz de nuestro fuego», while in the next two he confidently proclaims that their love can overcome harsh fate, thus resolving, to his own satisfaction at least, the two principal concerns or conflicts in the work: the poet has won his beloved, and both can defeat fate:

> Pues tan nacidamente soys vos mia,
> Yo vuestro soy, qual es del Sol el dia.
>     De aqui podeis hazer cierto argumento,
> Que contra nuestro Amor jamas ventura          250
> Tendra poder, pues tiene fundamento
> En la necessidad de la Natura:
> Siempre fue claro el Sol, mouible el Viento,
> Humida el Agua, fresca la verdura,
> Assi contra el cruel hado siniestro          255
> Vos siempre mia sereis, yo siempre vuestro.
>
> (132)

He also alludes here in a manner reminiscent of the opening of *Medoro y Angélica* and the conclusion of the *Otavas en diversas materias* to the Platonic doctrine of the necessity of love as though to set the seal on his assertion. The gradual attainment of this heady state is poetically convincing: it represents an apt means of detailing wishful thinking, or even self-delusion, if the poem is understood as the lover's capacity to read far more than has been promised into the lady's initial minimal favours. Supporting this approach or attitude is a tendency to pointed reasoning, as in stanza 16 with its sidesteps from supposition to fact. Underlying the whole process is the suggestion of an attempt to persuade by future expectation rather than present reality.

An identical situation is found in Herrera's *Elegía* III in which the poet reveals his joy at the beloved's readiness to speak with him. But though the situation is the same as in Aldana's *Otavas,* the approach is markedly different. The lady in Herrera's *Elegía* seems to acknowledge the poet's right to love her decorously and from a distance; on these terms she returns his love. [4] Aldana's poem is doubly different. Firstly, we learn very little about the lady herself: we gauge her reactions only through the poet's eyes and his view, as we have seen, is a partial and optimistic one. In Herrera's *Elegía,* the poet gives us the words of the lady herself. Secondly, in the *Otavas* there is a continuous consolidation of stages attained —a constant effort to go further and to overcome any obstacle encountered by the lover. In the *Elegía,* by contrast, there is a serene acceptance of the constraints attendant upon the concept of love as non-fulfilment and suffering. «Más ama quien más sufre y más padece» is the motto of the lover in Herrera's poem; Aldana's invokes the imperious dictate of «la necessidad de la Natura».

The *Otavas* end with the promise that the poet will commit what he has left unsaid to a letter:

> Todo aquello demas que yo dixera,
> Y escucharlo de vos por carta passe,
> Mi vida a Dios, quedad tan persuadida
> De mi, quanto de vos està mi vida.        264
>
> (133)

Whether this refers to the *Epístola a una dama cuyo principio falta* is not certain. While artistically fulfilling the unrealized promise of the *Otavas,* the *Epístola* is not obviously a sequel, although it has some emotional and expressive affinities with the other poem. Nowhere is the gulf between the two poems more evident than in the use of figurative language. In the following lines near the start of the *Epístola,* the poet enunciates the classic amatory relationship of Renaissance poetry. The lady overcomes the poet's soul; he has no will of his own; her rule is both terrible and fickle:

> Navío que en alto mar perdió la estrella
> es, de tan rico don desnuda, el alma,        5
> siendo la voluntad nueva alma della;
> tiene de mí la victoriosa palma
> otro querer, cual suele otro elemento
> distribüir al mar tormenta o calma;

---

[4] My view differs from that of R. O. Jones, who implies that the poet's love is fully reciprocated: «In *Elegía* III, he describes how Doña Leonor returned his love *in one unguarded moment*» (my italics). *A Literary History of Spain,* p. 97.

es el incontrastable mandamiento 10
de mi señora rayo presuroso
a quien se humilla y tiembla el firmamento.

(R, 43)

This is writing of a different class to that encountered in the *Otavas*. There is an intellectual rigour and control about the use of the figures of speech. Each of the three *tercetos* has a governing image: the first and third contain metaphors, the second a simile. The poet's soul is a ship that has lost its way; the beloved's domination of the lover is compared to the effect of the wind on the sea, by turns tempestuous and tranquil; the lady's commands are lightning-flashes of overwhelming power. These figures are not only closely related to each other but also seem to grow naturally from each other: the ship, the sea, the storm, or, more precisely, «navío», «mar», «tormenta», «rayo». So concentrated is this rationalization that the images do not seem embellishments; rather they appear to belong to the very essence of the experience —an impression not so dissimilar to that provided by Ausiàs March's emotive use of simile.

The opening *terceto* also has an intensity of expression that is nowhere evident in the *Otavas:*

¡Ay dura ley de amor que así me obliga
a no tener más voluntad de aquella
que me ordena el rigor de mi enemiga!

(43)

After outlining the situation in which he finds himself, the poet refers to a prohibition placed on him by the beloved: he must not unburden himself or complain to her of his suffering («me impide el descubrirme»), while she, for her part, can both destroy him and yet remain detached. This is a standard amatory pose,[5] but it has seldom been as powerfully or concisely rendered as this:

mas quiere que no pueda y que no quiera 20
y mata y, tras matar, niega herirme.

(44)

The poet sees no alternative other than to fulfill this command:

y pues desnudo estoy de la potencia 25
para negar, conviértase mi vida
en alta ejecución de la sentencia.

(44)

---

[5] Compare, for example, QUEVEDO's sonnet «¿Qué importa blasonar del albedrío» (ed. cit., p. 491). See my observations on this and other similar poems in WALTERS, *Francisco de Quevedo, Love Poet*, pp. 82-84.

The first part of the poem concludes with the lover's melancholy resignation to his fate and an affirmation of his perseverance in loving:

> ¡Ay, que el que ve a un miserable amante
> vivir, morir y amar, luego se inflama
> de celo en tanto ardor firme y constante!     39
>
> (44)

The last tercet of this section then begins with an exclamation (¡ay!) as had the first of the poem. Perhaps this is an indication that, contrary to what the title states, there is no missing material at the start of the poem. Indeed in this, as in other aspects, the poem has a purposeful, compact quality far removed from the prolixity and repetitiveness of the *Otavas*.

    The greater sense of direction in the *Epístola* manifests itself in the linear progression of the argument; there is not that constant recapitulation that characterizes the *Otavas*. That a new issue arises at line 40 is clearly marked:

> Mas nueva voz me acude y me reclama,     40
> dentro del más secreto pensamiento,
> que rompedor de fe me nombra y llama,
>     diciendo: «El mandamiento y juramento
> rompes de no escribir antes ni agora
> la causa y ocasión de tu tormento.»     45
>
> (44)

A note of defiance is struck here. The poet refers to what seems like a challenge to the uncompromising dictates of his mistress; the phrases «secreto pensamiento» and «rompedor de fe» add to the feeling of rebelliousness. What this amounts to is the poet's rejection of the prohibition imposed upon him: to maintain silence, he argues, would be disobedient, hence he writes. Furthermore, he writes to show his compliance to the lady's will, and not to offend her nor, paradoxically, to write to her. The mode of reasoning is particularly insidious and a decidedly ambivalent impression is provided. This kind of sophistry verges on irreverence and it certainly hints at a tongue-in-cheek approach:

> pues si te escribo, es solo por decirte
> que ella obedecerá cuanto quisieres,     50
> y no por ofenderte ni escribirte...
>
> (44)

There follows a vehement assertion of the lover's wish to be obedient to his lady come what may, though the reader may not take such sentiments at face value in the light of previous reasoning:

> Y así de nuevo torno a consagrarte     55
> la dada fe, que nunca desconcierte
> del punto adonde está por observarte;

> puede muy bien la inexorable muerte
> romper la nueva estambre de mi vida,
> mas no el deseo de siempre obedecerte.            60
>
> (45)

After elaborating at some length on his good intentions and making much
of his loyalty (the word «fe» is employed several times), the lover takes the
liberty of proposing an amendment, or at least an addition, to the lady's
stipulation:

> Y porque no la cubra ciego olvido
> de vil costumbre, bien será que quede
> esto por ley de amor establecido...            75
>
> (45)

The word «ley» harks back to the opening of the poem where the lover had
complained of the «dura ley de amor». But subtly and gradually he has been
establishing an alternative «law»:

> pues siempre renovar se me concede
> la escrita fe, que en el discurso humano
> tanto, con Dios, y en ti tan poco puede;
> y tú también, con más piadoso y llano
> trato, me escribirás que yo confirme            80
> la nueva obligación de propria mano...
>
> (45)

Not only is it right and proper («lawful» even in the terms in which this
amatory relationship seems to be conceived) that the poet should write, but,
in addition, that he should do so repeatedly and that the lady should also
write in reply and in a less hostile fashion than she has treated him hitherto.
This represents a striking departure from the picture painted in the first part
of the poem with its emphasis on the poet's helplessness and enslavement.
The reference in line 83 to the lady's power («por usar tu cetro y mando»)
recalls the description of her awesome control at the start of the poem, but
in the new dispensation it is ironic for it is the lover who now has the ini-
tiative.

At this juncture the lover again feels the need for self-justification. He
has recourse to an extended metaphor in order to illustrate the point that
although he has refashioned the amatory law, he has not diluted its effec-
tiveness:

> No porque el fuerte pino, al comenzarse
> de su nueva raíz, si un brazo estiende,
> deja con mil raíces de arraigarse,
> con quien después se ampara y se defiende
> del riguroso y descortés invierno,            95
> que apenas hoja de él daña y ofende;

tu mandamiento así, pues, blando y tierno
dentro mi pecho está cual niño en cuna,
conservando el poder largo y eterno
    para que el tiempo, al fin, muerte, y fortuna,           100
caso, destino, providencia y arte
no me puedan entrar en suerte alguna.

(46)

A telling stylistic touch here is the way in which the metaphor with its
majestic subject and treatment yields to the concise simplicity and tenderness of the simile. The final *terceto* of this quotation recalls the *Otavas en
diversa materia.* The poet refers to how secure the *amada*'s command is
with him; it will be immune to the ravages of time and fate. He also implies that it is, in a sense, a safeguard since «no me puedan entrar» —an
idea that is reminiscent of the assumption in the *Otavas* that the shared
love of the poet and the beloved can defeat misfortune. In the *Epístola,* the
«mandamiento» does not, at first sight, amount to the same as a presumed
reciprocated love but as the underlying meanings and motives of the poem
become more apparent, it will be evident that a similar approach and similar
processes are at play. A few lines below, the poet again makes use of metaphor in order to demonstrate his sincerity and straightforwardness. It would
have seemed from earlier passages that these were hardly the most salient
qualities displayed by the lover and the very contours of the passage itself
serve to confirm this impression:

No tiene mi verdad sincera y pura,
cierta, abundante, y de sí misma llena,           110
necesidad de ajena compostura:
    sería de Libia a la quemada arena
agua pedir el húmido Oceano
y a la ortiga su olor el azucena,
    del seco invierno el dulce abril temprano       115
flores coger, y la desierta cumbre
de hierba enriquecer al fértil llano;
    robar el claro sol belleza y lumbre
a la noche sería más triste y fea,
y el mundo renovar suerte y costumbre.       120

(47)

The poet states that he does not need to be affected or extravagant in af-
firming the truth of what he says and feels, but then unfolds a series of
images that illustrate what he need *not* do. Having explicitly eschewed extravagance («ajena compostura») he then indulges in it. By the repetition of
«verdad» in the line immediately following the last one quoted above, the
lover seems to «protest too much». By now the reader will surely be fully
alive to the layer of challenge and rebellion present in the poem. After an
address to the *amada,* couched in standard Petrarchist terms (ll. 121-38), the

poem aptly concludes with an assertion that in the light of all that has been said is hard to accept at face value:

> Quédese, pues, aquí mi dolorosa
> y baja pluma sólo con decirte                                    140
> que mientras no mandares otra cosa,
> siempre te serviré de no escribirte.
>
> (48)

In view of the poet's aim to point or even twist words and meaning it is appropriate that he should have chosen the establishing of law as his governing metaphor. Moreover, there are numerous instances of a kind of phraseology that is reminiscent of legal jargon, involving pleonastic rationalizations in such phrases as «que así quiero y que quisiera» (l. 22), «pues forzosa piedad me tiene y debe» (l. 32) and «sólo porque tengas y poseas» (l. 67).[6] Such processes also occur in longer passages, for example:

> Mas nueva voz *me acude y me reclama,*                           40
> dentro del más secreto pensamiento,
> que rompedor de fe me *nombra y llama,*
>     diciendo: *«El mandamiento y juramento*
> rompes de no escribir antes ni agora
> *la causa y ocasión* de tu tormento.»                            45
>
> (44) (my italics)

> con quien después *se ampara y se defiende*
> del *riguroso y descortés* invierno,                             95
> que apenas hoja de el *daña y ofende...*
>
> (46) (my italics)

> a pecho que es de amor *guarida y puerto,*
> a frente de valor tan *rica y llena,*                            125
> cualquier cerrado abismo es aire abierto.
>
> (47) (my italics)

Consistent with such a procedure is the sophistry displayed at the start of the second section of the poem and an occasionally surprising and ironic use of language. For instance, in these lines:

> Entiende, pues, hermosa usurpadora
> de mi albedrío, cuan libre, sin mentirte,
> está de culpa el alma que te adora...                            48
>
> (44)

---

[6] ALFREDO LEFEBVRE (*La poesía del capitán Aldana,* p. 173) draws attention to a similar procedure in the *Carta para Arias Montano,* e.g. «un hombre desvalido y bajo», «Oficio militar profeso y hago». What gives it added significance in the *Epístola* is the presence of law (specifically «leyes») as a crucial metaphor.

the word «libre» momentarily surprises us because it occurs immediately after an opposite concept —that of the enslavement of the lover's free-will. This unexpected impression is created by inversion: by the delay of the subject of the clause. A similar sensation is produced by the use of the word «deseo» in these lines:

> puede muy bien la inexorable muerte
> romper la nueva estambre de mi vida,
> mas no el deseo de siempre obedecerte...          60
>
> (45)

For a moment, as the word is initially registered, the reader may think in terms of desire as a wish for fulfilment; the full phrase, however, suggests that it is the opposite of this, i. e., the wish (desire) to obey the *amada*. But in view of the ambivalence of the poet's obedience, the initial impression —that of erotic aspiration— may well reassert itself. In this connection it may be worth quoting the unusual verb employed at the end of the section in which the poet has been refashioning the lovers' law:

> y así, la fe y el mando repitiendo,
> imposible será después quebrarse
> tan alta convención cual voy tejiendo.          90
>
> (46)

The poet uses the metaphor of weaving, suggestive perhaps of intricacy and cunning. The ultimate purpose of such a devious use of words and reasoning will be apparent by now. It resides in the poet's attempt to seduce his beloved. The poem could be interpreted as a response to the challenge posed by the demands outlined at the start of the work. Thus the poem resembles *Medoro y Angélica* and the *Otavas en diversa materia* in its expression both of the lover's frustration and of his efforts to overcome it. Certainly, the poet in the *Epístola* betrays both irreverence and an eagerness to respond to the challenge, and in some instances his true intentions are all but transparent. Again the choice of diction is important. In the following lines from the first part of the poem, the lover speaks of his inability to resist the commands of the lady. This is expressed in unusual and pointed terms:

> y pues desnudo estoy de la potencia          25
> para negar, conviértase mi vida
> en alta ejecución de la sentencia...
>
> (44)

Significantly there appear the words «desnudo» and «potencia» whose erotic association is obvious.[7] What gives added piquancy again is that the

---

[7] It does not seem unlikely that Quevedo had these lines in mind when he wrote a sonnet to Lisi on the frustrations of the lover unable to communicate his emotions

context in which these words figure concerns the denial of what the primary associations of the words suggest. Such a tension serves as an appropriate correlative when we discover that the poet has no intention of obeying the lady's command.

The *Epístola* perhaps owes more to the *cancionero* tradition than any other of Aldana's compositions, except possibly for the two poems to be considered below. The word-play and polyptoton of these lines offer a particularly good example of the *cancionero* style:

> Perder la voluntad caso es lloroso,
> mas, ¿cómo llora aquel que para el llanto,
> sin ajeno poder, no es poderoso? 15
> ¡Estrañeza de amor digna de espanto,
> que tras tan largo mal sin resentirme,
> quiere que el mismo mal no sienta tanto!
>
> (43)

But the *cancionero* influence is important too for another reason. It is that the ambivalence, challenge and veiled eroticism of the work are features that one critic, at least, has seen as hallmarks of *cancionero* poetry. Keith Whinnom has argued persuasively that many words in *cancionero* verse have a hidden erotic significance beneath their superficially innocent appearance. [8] Contributing to this effect is the tendency to make use of abstract, very generalized terms. Whinnom has also compiled from various sources a list of verbs that refer to the sexual act (p. 36), and among these is one that is a dominant one in the *Epístola* —«escribir». It is to be found, for example, in an anonymous *villancico*, published in the *Tercera parte de flor de romances* in Madrid in 1593 and later included in the *Romancero general*. The poem uses the metaphor of scholarly apprenticeship for sexual activity as the following lines make clear:

> Donde vee hermosas damas
> da liciones, aunque aprende,
> y con sus letras enciende
> en sus pechos vivas llamas;
> y quiere sobre las camas
> dar liciones y tomar... [9]

In this context the obscene significance of what follows is obvious:

---

to his mistress. He muses on the delights that would accrue to him if only his eyelids were lips:

> De invisible comercio mantenidos,
> y desnudos de cuerpo, los favores
> gozaran mis potencias y sentidos.
>
> (*Ed. cit.*, p. 495)

[8] *La poesía amatoria*, p. 34.
[9] Printed in *Poesía erótica del Siglo de Oro*, ed. PIERRE ALZIEU, ROBERT JAMMES, YVAN LISSORGUES (Barcelona: Editorial Crítica, 1984), p. 87.

Y trae consigo la pluma,
que quiere escribir primero,
y echa tinta en el tintero
de lo que della rezuma...

(ll. 21-24)

When we remember that Aldana's poem revolves around the question of
whether the lover should be allowed to write or not, and when we recall
the importance he attaches to that action then perhaps the verb «escribir»
has something of the secondary, erotic meaning of the poem quoted above.
The seeming contradiction of the following *terceto* lends support, in my
view, to such an interpretation:

pues si te escribo, es sólo por decirte
que ella obedecerá cuanto quisieres,                                        50
y no por ofenderte ni escribirte...

(44)

It could be that «escribo» in the first line of this quotation bears a literal
meaning, while «escribirte» in the third has an obscene, metaphorical significance, especially as it is juxtaposed with the idea of giving offence. In
fact, it could be argued that these lines are fully understood only if we are
prepared to accept the existence of two levels of meaning; in this way, there
is no contradiction.

It might not be entirely fanciful either to suggest that a phrase at the
very end of the poem:

Quédese, pues, aquí mi dolorosa
y baja pluma...                                                          140

(48)

has a secondary, graphic significance, in which «pluma» is understood as
a phallic symbol. This is, of course, a tentative rather than a definitive interpretation; and to take such an approach to an extreme by reading an erotic
or obscene layer of meaning in every line or idea of the poem would be an
absurd exaggeration. Nonetheless, the secondary significance of words like
«escribir» and «pluma» are not to be dismissed, especially as the whole poem
is so clearly an expression of defiance and challenge; that it contains a secondary *intent* —to overcome the obstacles of the lady's hostility— is evident.
In conclusion, I would suggest that the role of the secondary meanings in
the *Epístola* should be assessed along the same lines as those specified by
Whinnom when he discusses the presence of such terminology in *cancionero*
poetry:

No estoy dispuesto a sostener que, cuando los poetas cancioneriles se que-
jan: «Y muero porque no muero», están diciendo abiertamente: «Siento do-
lores mortales porque mi amada no me permite el alivio sexual», sino que de-

69

trás de la paradoja del vivo muerto, de la que se podrían citar múltiples ejemplos, yace también esta sugerencia erótica. [10]

The *Redondillas discontinuadas* provides another example of Aldana's *cancionero*-inspired poetry, but constitutes an altogether slighter and more frivolous composition than the *Epístola*. As so often the title is misleading for the poem seems all of a piece. It depends for its effect on the insistent play on the phrase «no quiero» uttered by the lady. It is mainly treated as a noun as in the second line of the poem:

> Tan dulcemente profiere
> Vn no quiero mi Señora
> Y el mismo assi me enamora
> Que otro no quiero no quiere,
> Mi Alma en qualquiera hora.          5
>
> (OC, II, 191)

This opening is reminiscent of the *canción* «El mayor bien de quereros» by Diego de San Pedro, which begins as follows:

> El mayor bien de quereros
> es querer un no quererme,
> pues procurar de perderos
> será perder el perderme. [11]

Aldana is neither as subtle nor as concise as the earlier poet; after a while, his wordiness and repetitiveness start to pall. The poem is an exercise in the *cancionero* manner rather than an assimilation and recreation of its characteristic stylistic and thematic piquancies. Nevertheless, the poet again probes the erotic levels latent in this tradition, as in the use of the term «gozo cumplido» at the end of one stanza, hinting at something far bolder than has yet been achieved:

> Pues quando siento deziros
> No quiero, todo en oydo
> Querria boluer, y el sentido,
> Abiuar por mas ohiros,
> Por tener gozo cumplido.          25
>
> (192)

and in the sensual implications of the imagery in the third stanza:

> Deue ser que en vuestra boca
> Nectar ay, y Ambrosia pura,
> Pues que conuierte en dulçura
> Como Abeja lo que toca,
> Y le quita su amargura.          15
>
> (191)

---

[10] *La poesía amatoria*, p. 37.
[11] As edited by WHINNOM, *La poesía amatoria*, p. 74.

For my final illustration of Aldana's *cancionero* manner and its use in a context of covert and insidious aspiration I turn to his *soneto* XX. This poem has as its mainspring the contrast of «bien» and «mal», favoured terms in *cancionero* poetry. A key word in this sonnet, however, and one which, in my view, has led to its being misunderstood is «cuidado» in line two:

> Es tanto el bien que derramó en mi seno,
> piadoso de mi mal, vuestro cuidado,
> que nunca fué, tras mal, bien tan preciado
> como este tal, por mí de bien tan lleno.
> Mal que este bien causó jamás ajeno
> sea de mí ni de mí quede apartado;
> antes, del cuerpo al alma trasladado,
> se reserve de muerte un mal tan bueno.
> Mas paréceme ver que el mortal velo,
> no consintiendo al mal nuevo aposento,
> lo guarda allá en su centro el más profundo;
> sea, pues, así: que el cuerpo acá en el suelo
> posea su mal, y al postrimero aliento
> gócelo el alma y pase a nuevo mundo.
>
> (R, 14)

Rivers is of the opinion that the sonnet was inspired by an injury or wound suffered by the lover and which attracted the sympathy of the lady.[12] This is to read «cuidado» too narrowly and too literally in the context of six-teenth-century love poetry. «Cuidado» is a term often used as a synonym for love or even, more generally, emotion. It has the latter significance in stanza 13 of the *Otavas en diversa materia:*

> Vendra mi propia vida à ser mi muerte
> Viniendo a ser en mi vuestro cuydado
> De mas rigor, mas poderosa, y fuerte
> Como rayo del Sol reuerberado...        100
>
> (OC, II, 125)

In one of Giovanni della Casa's sonnets where the idea of illness and healing is used as an amatory metaphor we find a kind of terminology («mal», «cura», «salute») similar to that in Aldana's poem:

> Quella che del mio mal cura non prende,
> come colpa non sia de' suoi begli occhi
> quant'io languisco, o come altronde scocchi
> l'acuto stral che la mia vita offende;
> non gradisce il mio cor e no 'l mi rende,
> perch'ei sempre di lacrime trabocchi:
> né vòl ch'i' pèra; e perché già mi tocchi
> morte col braccio, ancor non mi difende.

[12] *Poesías*, p. 14n.

71

E io son preso ed è 'l carcer aperto:
e giungo a mia salute e fuggo indietro:
e gioia 'n forse bramo e duol ho certo.
    Da spada di diamante un fragil vetro
schermo mi face, e di mio stato incerto
né morte, Amor, da te, né vita impetro. [13]

It would thus seem quite permissible to read Aldana's sonnet as a poem in which the lover expresses his joy at having his love returned. «Bien» would represent fulfilment, «mal», his past frustration and desires, and «cuidado», the beloved's amorous attention. The striking phrase «derramó en mi seno» would be appropriate for the physical pleasure afforded the poet, and «piadoso» would be an euphemism for the lady's willingness to return the poet's love. Nothing in this interpretation is novel or fanciful given the ambiguous potential of the words employed. But I cannot wholeheartedly subscribe to this analysis for from the seventh line onwards the poet unexpectedly introduces a new line of thought that does not readily tally with the opening. The argument seems to proceed as follows: so desirable is the «mal» that could give rise to «bien» (indeed that necessarily must precede «bien» if «mal» is understood as desire) that the poet would wish to keep it forever, even beyond death. For this to happen it would need to pass from the temporal part, his body, to the eternal part, the soul. But it seems that the body is unwilling for this to happen; it is, presumably, jealous of the boon it enjoys and so the poet concludes by accepting that his body should entertain the «bien» while he is alive and that it should transfer to his soul at the moment of death when he enters a new existence. The basis for this mode of reasoning is of course Neoplatonic but it seems here an unnecessarily ponderous recourse for expressing the paradox that the «bien» exists only because there was previously a «mal» or, in my interpretation, that fulfilment requires prior desire, even allowing for the poet-lover's characteristic hyperbole. Whatever view one takes of the sonnet, there appears to be no satisfactory explanation for the turn it takes around mid-poem, and the safest, if slightly harsh, conclusion is that the poet, as in other places, is experimenting: attempting, in this instance, to blend *cancionero* terminology with a Neoplatonic approach. The outcome is a poem that is intriguing rather than convincing, although Aldana's failures or relative failures have an attractive quality that outlives the successes of lesser poets.

The abiding impression of Aldana's love poetry is restlessness and vitality. The lover seems to live with the notion of ever-present and imminent change: at the moment of fulfilment, there is an awareness of loss and dissatisfaction. Conversely, even when rejected and frustrated, the lover hopes

---

[13] *Poesia italiana del Cinquecento*, p. 115.

and schemes for the achievement of his goal. Other poets of Aldana's era wrote of the transience of human love and the mutability of emotion, but by comparison with Aldana in a way that seems restrained, even static. Few Spanish poets of any age have captured as well as he the dynamic energy that informs passion and the sense of emotion not only in being but somehow in movement, constantly becoming.

# 5

# ON PHILOSOPHY AND FRIENDSHIP:
## THE VERSE EPISTLES

The creative restlessness that characterizes Aldana's love poetry is also a hallmark of his verse epistles. No two of these six poems are alike, either in content or in structure and together they serve as a compendium of the genre in the Golden Age. But they are not merely representative. In scope and intention they mark an advance, bringing to the genre a richness and dignity unparalleled in Renaissance poetry and without precedent in classical literature. Furthermore, contrary to received opinion, this achievement is not confined to a single poem. Although the *Carta para Arias Montano* has monopolized critical acclaim, the other epistles have striking features both of form and content that warrant analytic attention.

The variety of these poems is such that two of them — the *Epístola a una dama* and the *Carta para Arias Montano* — are discussed in other chapters. There is, additionally, variety of metre: three poems are written in *tercetos,* three in blank verse. This equal division is unusual. The form favoured for epistolary verse by Garcilaso's contemporaries and immediate successors was the *terceto,* an Italianate form corresponding to the *terza rima,* a metre appropriate for the extended composition. Blank verse tended to be employed for genres other than the epistolary, notably for the mythological poem as with Boscán's *Leandro y Hero* and Acuña's *Contienda de Áyax Telemanio y de Ulises sobre las armas de Aquiles.* Introduced into Italian literature by Trissino in his play *Sofonisba* in 1515, it subsequently became employed in poetry as an equivalent for the unrhymed hexameter.[1] The first poem written in blank verse in Spanish was a verse epistle, Garcilaso's *Epístola a Boscán,* in all probability inspired by recently-published poems of Alamanni.[2] More influential for the first generation of Spanish Petrarchists, however, were the

---

[1] For the rationale behind Trissino's adoption of blank verse, see JOHN A. SCOTT'S observations in *The Continental Renaissance,* p. 252; and E. H. WILKINS, *A History of Italian Literature* (Cambridge, Massachusetts: Harvard University Press, 1974), pp. 238-40.

[2] This is suggested by HAYWARD KENISTON, *Garcilaso de la Vega: A Critical Study of his Life and Works* (New York: Hispanic Society of America, 1922), p. 337.

epistles in *tercetos* that Garcilaso entitled *Elegías*. The *Epístola* is a modest poem in dimension and intention and can hardly have been a structural model for Aldana's ambitious verse epistles despite some evidence of lexical influence on his *Respuesta a Cosme*. Aldana's blank-verse epistles combine in a unique way the *verso suelto* metre with the more or less standard content and structural sophistication of those epistles written in *tercetos*.

Aldana's three epistles in *tercetos* deal with amatory, moral and philosophical concerns respectively. The *Epístola a una dama*, as we have seen, is in the tradition of *cancionero*-inspired love poetry of the sixteenth century, whose diction and terminology, though not its approach, recall those poems from Book Three of Boscán's works written in *tercetos:* the *Capítulo* and the *Epístola*. Herrera's *Elegías* belong to the same sub-grouping of amatory compositions employing this metre. The *Carta para Arias Montano,* as we shall see, restores to the poem in *tercetos* a dignity, indeed a sublimity, that it had lacked in the work of Italian poets in particular in the *Cinquecento*. With this poem of Aldana there is a sobriety of tone and movement more in keeping with the *Divina Commedia* and the *Trionfi* than with the satirical and frivolous *capitoli* of Francesco Berni. In terms of sixteenth-century poetic theory, having regard for the theory of decorum, the difference is one between an «elevated» and a «base» style. Although Spanish poets by and large eschewed the burlesque poem in *tercetos,* neither did they adopt it for such lofty poetry as the *Carta para Arias Montano*. They reserved it for two kinds of poetry, both of which correspond to what according to the principle of decorum would be termed the «mean» style: pastoral and moral verse — the more serious kinds of lyric poetry.[3] In both, the communicative intent is important. In the pastoral, the *terceto* is employed for soliloquies and dialogue as in Garcilaso's *Eclogue* II and Acuña's *Égloga*, «Con nuevo resplandor Febo salía». In the case of moral poetry, the *terceto* was used for what has been called the Horatian epistle —a letter in verse addressed to a friend, combining informality of manner with observations of a philosophical nature. This sub-genre continued to be popular into the seventeenth century as evidenced by well-known poems by Andrada *(Epístola moral a Fabio)* and Quevedo *(Epístola satírica y censoria)*. The pioneering works had been the letters in verse exchanged between Hurtado de Mendoza and Boscán. Aldana is different in that he uses blank verse rather than *tercetos* for such epistles. He appears to have considered the *terceto* better suited to the more formal kind of communication than did other poets. This is especially true of the epistle in *tercetos* yet to be considered — the *Pocos tercetos escritos a un amigo*.

---

[3] For an account of the application of the principle of decorum see *An Anthology of Spanish Poetry 1500-1700. Part One: 1500-1580,* ed. ARTHUR TERRY (Oxford: Pergamon, 1965), pp. xxi-xxii.

This poem stands apart from the other verse epistles even allowing for the heterogeneous nature of the group as a whole. It is very obviously the shortest of the set. Moreover it is stylized in form and impersonal in tone: both the «yo» and the friend are assigned conventionally-prescribed roles as opposite extremes in an antithesis. In the other verse epistles the moral element emerges naturally from an informal or at least relaxed discourse, but in *Pocos tercetos* it forms the whole body of the poem, which is, effectively, a single premise. It possesses then a structural severity and argumentative rigidity far removed from the apparent spontaneity of the blank-verse epistles. It comprises an extended antithesis based on a repeated syntactical formula of a temporal clause, introduced by «mientras», followed by the main clause. The contrast is between the military and the courtly, activities which are associated with the poet and the addressee respectively. In the odd-numbered tercets the subordinate clause describes the effete pleasures of courtly life; the even-numbered ones, consisting of the main clause, offer a strikingly opposite picture of the rigours of a soldier's existence. Although Aldana relates the harshness of military life more memorably in other places, the poem in *tercetos* is impressive because of its imaginative pinpointing of details for the purpose of comparison. The effect is one of balance: one word or phrase from one part of the dichotomy countered by a corresponding one in the other part. Such a technique has an influence on the register of the poem by supplying an implicit judgement. The attitude is nearer reproach than friendship or admiration, another trait that differentiates it from the other verse epistles. The first sentence is a case in point:

> Mientras estáis allá con tierno celo,
> de oro, de seda y púrpura cubriendo
> el de vuestra alma vil terrestre velo,
>     sayo de hierro acá yo estoy vistiendo,
> cota de acero, arnés, yelmo luciente,                    5
> que un claro espejo al sol voy pareciendo.
>
> (R, 55)

There is here, as elsewhere in the poem, a clear semantic-structural parallel: the second line of both tercets describes items of clothing and has a tripartite structure. A more pointed comparison occurs between the third lines. The pejorative circumlocution for the body, underscored by an ugly hyperbaton (1. 3), is offset by the simile in the main clause (1. 6) that invites us to see the soldier's armour as a mirror for the sun, an ennobling image much favoured by Aldana as a positive, even transcendental signifier. The lexical antitheses («terrestre»-«sol»; «vil»-«claro») underline the poet's polemical approach, suggesting judgement by such precise focussing.

The second sentence similarly contains specific contrasts:

Mientras andáis allá lascivamente
con flores de azahar, con agua clara
los pulsos refrescando, ojos y frente,
 yo de honroso sudor cubro mi cara    10
y de sangre enemiga el brazo tiño
cuando con más furor muerte dispara.

(55)

The «agua clara» associated with the courtier is opposed by the «sudor» of the soldier, but semantically linked by the element of liquid. Likewise one can detect the same process of opposite but related significance in the visual congruity of «sangre» and «flores». The contrast of such qualifying words as «lascivamente» and «honroso» in the first line of the two clauses further serves to sharpen our judgement.

The fourth sentence contains an arresting antithesis that involves the use of names:

Mientras andáis allá con la memoria
llena de las blanduras de Cupido,    20
publicando de vos llorosa historia,
 yo voy acá de furia combatido,
de aspereza y desdén, lleno de gana
que Ludovico al fin quede vencido.

(56)

While the courtier-friend pursues activities associated with love, specifically Cupid, the poet-soldier is engaged in deadly pursuit of a real figure, Count Louis de Nassau-Dillenburg, who, in 1568, fought against the Spanish armies in the Low Countries. The phonetic resemblance between the two names, similar in assonance *(u-i-o)* provides an impression of bathos. By thus deflating the courtly aspect the poet is able to enhance the military.

The final sentence contains a witty contrast, arising from a comparison of love and war:

Mientras andáis allá metido todo
en conocer la dama, o linda o fea,
buscando introducción por diestro modo,
 yo reconozco el sitio y la trinchea
deste profano a Dios vil enemigo,    35
sin que la muerte al ojo estorbo sea.

(56)

As the courtier seeks to win over the lady by stealth and subtlety so too does the soldier strive by his patience to defeat the «vil enemigo». The contrast is built on a point of similarity in the shape of a commonplace of amatory ideology found frequently in Medieval allegories: the lover laying siege to his obdurate mistress. In this analogy, as with the «sangre»-«flores» comparison, Aldana anticipates the conceits Góngora was to employ in his *romances*. [4] More generally, the technique of comparing dissimilar objects or ideas, of finding likeness in things that are unlike, is precisely that considered to be a hallmark of the Metaphysical Poets. [5]

The *Pocos tercetos* then have nothing of the relaxed, extempore manner which is one of the attributes of epistolary verse and which is present even in the majestic outlines of the *Carta para Arias Montano*. For a blending of impromptu approach and structural design we have to turn to the blank-verse epistles where the formal and the flexible are, on the whole, successfully integrated.

In some respects, however, this is not such an unlikely combination. It is important to recognize that recourse to a quasi-colloquial style and the adoption of a casual manner do not preclude certain conventions. Indeed within the genre of the verse epistle one can identify a number of *topoi*. There is, firstly, an acknowledgement of the addressee. Occasionally this entails the naming of the recipient of the letter at the start, as in Garcilaso's *Elegía* II and *Epístola a Boscán*, Hurtado de Mendoza's *Epístola a Boscán* and Aldana's own *Carta para Arias Montano*. This procedure could be seen as corresponding to the heading of letters. There is, likewise, an equivalent for the ending and signature in the poet's indication of place and date. This can take the form of a straightforward reference, as at the end of the *Carta para Arias Montano*:

> De Madrid a los siete de setiembre,        450
> mil y quinientos y setenta y siete.
>
> (74)

or a periphrastic rendering, as with Garcilaso's *Epístola a Boscán*:

> Doce del mes d'otubre, de la tierra
> do nació el claro fuego del Petrarcha
> y donde están del fuego las cenizas.
>
> (11. 83-85)

and Aldana's *Carta a Galanio*:

> De la Ciudad que dista siete leguas
> De la yglesia mayor, que hay en Castilla.
> A los 7 del mes, que el Sol discurre        525
> El signo que tambien acaba en siete
> Tomando del Carnero a los Pescados.
>
> (OC, I, 220)

---

[4] See in particular the *romances* beginning «Entre los sueltos caballos», «Servía en Orán al Rey», «En un pastoral albergue».
[5] See *The Metaphysical Poets*, 2nd ed., ed. HELEN GARDNER (Harmondsworth: Penguin, 1966), pp. 19-22.

Another common feature of the verse epistle is the acknowledgement of a letter from the recipient. Such a letter may actually exist as with the correspondence between Hurtado de Mendoza and Boscán. On other occasions, however, there is no record of the letter to which reference is made. It may be that the recipient's letter has been lost. Alternatively, it is possible that it never existed: that the author of the verse epistle refers to it as a conventional device in order to serve the design of his own poem. Such may be the case, as we shall see, with the letter referred to in the *Carta a Galanio.*

Conventional too is the attitude of the poet towards the receptor. In this the *Pocos tercetos* were untypical as the tone of address is normally respectful and imbued with modesty. Such an approach manifests itself in various ways. Sometimes the poet laments what he considers to be an ungainly style. In this the verse epistle recalls the assumption of modesty in the pastoral as, for example, when Garcilaso in his *Eclogue* III refers to the «bajo son de mi zampoña ruda, / indigna de llegar a tus oídos» (ll. 42-43). In the same poet's *Epístola a Boscán* there is a significant variation of this idea. He justifies the colloquial style of the poem because it is more appropriate to an intimate letter:

> ni será menester buscar estilo
> presto, distinto d'ornamento puro
> tal cual a culta epístola conviene.

> (11. 5-7)

In his *Carta al Señor Don Bernardino de Mendoza,* Aldana combines the modesty pose with an encomium of the recipient, contrasting his own cumbersome attempts at letter-writing — «las digresiones / que hago» (ll. 67-68); «Doctrina en versos» (1. 72) — with the clarity and poise of the letter he has received.

Another topic involves the poet regretting his delay in replying, sometimes because of his inability to begin his letter. Such is the excuse offered by Cetina at the opening of his poem to the Príncipe de Áscoli:

> Señor, más de cien veces he tomado
> la pluma y el papel para escribiros,
> y tantas no sé cómo lo he dejado.

In his *Respuesta a Cosme,* Aldana expands upon this *topos.* He states how difficult he finds it to start his reply and merges this idea with the theme of lost poetic inspiration:

> Al fin, venido aquí, tomé la pluma
> para estender con más limado estilo
> tanta del alma alteración secreta,
> mas ¡ay, que mil y mil, mil y mil vueltas
> hice principio, y cuatro mil tras ellas          70
> borré el principio, que sin gracia entraba!

¡Oh dulce musa mía!, ¿cómo y qué es esto?
Pues cómo, ¿no solías, mi dulce musa,
de aquel celeste ardor toda inflamada
con que a tu Galatea fuiste agradable,                                    75
cantar tan dulcemente que juraba
la misma Galatea sobre sus ojos
(¡oh dulzura especial de juramento!),
so pena de perdellos, que no había
musa oído jamás de mejor gusto?                                           80

(R, 51)

Verse epistles partook of convention in the matter of content as well as style. As Rivers has noted, the Horatian epistle —the source for sixteenth-century Spanish poets— combined the form of the personal letter with a philosophic component.[6] This did not usually appear as a coherent system but rather as a flexible body of ideas. Such a procedure reflects Horace's own eclecticism, drawing freely as he did on Stoic and Epicurean writers. By the same token Spanish poets blended Horatian material with contemporary commonplaces such as the scorn of the city and praise of the country. Indeed, even as early as Boscán, the Horatian element acquires accretions in the shape of *Cortesano* and Christian ideas.[7] Such a practice foreshadows Aldana's intentions in the *Carta para Arias Montano,* overlaid as it is with Christian Neoplatonism.

The influence of Horace extended to specific lexical areas. Thus the favourite notion of the Golden Mean *(aurea mediocritas)* and the desire to attain happiness by the avoidance of vice is manifested in the prominence of words like «medio» and «virtud» and related terms in the epistles of Garcilaso, Boscán, Hurtado de Mendoza and, also, in Aldana's blank-verse epistles. This aspect of Horace's thought would have proved especially attractive to sixteenth-century poets because of its similarity to Aristotelian ideas. In particular, the *Nicomachean Ethics,* the work that most influenced the moral thinking of Renaissance writers, discusses at length the nature of virtue — both intellectual and ethical — and essays a definition by considering it a mean between the vices of excess and defect.[8] Aldana, one of the most philosophically-orientated poets of the Golden Age, exploited Aristotelian «virtud» in a structural as well as thematic fashion in his *Carta a Don Bernardino de Mendoza.*

Other works of Aristotle and Aristotelians left a clear imprint on Aldana's epistles. In both the *Respuesta a Cosme* and the *Carta a Galanio* there is near the start of the poem a lengthy account of the workings of the imagi-

---

[6] «The Horatian Epistle and its Introduction into Spanish Literature», *Hispanic Review,* 22 (1954), 175-94 (at p. 181).

[7] See ARNOLD G. REICHENBERGER, «Boscán's *Epístola a Mendoza*», *Hispanic Review,* 17 (1949), 1-17.

[8] See Book B (1107A). I have drawn on the edition by HIPPOCRATES G. APOSTLE (Dordrecht: D. Reidel, 1975).

nation derived from Aristotle's *De anima* (III, 3). An extract from the *Respuesta a Cosme* gives an indication of how detailed the exposition is. It relates how the recollection of his brother suddenly came upon the poet:

                cuando, sin advertir, hete en el alma                          5
                un trueno disparar, hete que veo
                un relámpago dar con presta vuelta
                inusitado asalto a la memoria:
                el sentido exterior quedó turbado,
                luego el común revuelve las especies                        10
                y a la imaginación las da y entrega,
                la cual, después, con más delgado examen,
                hace a la fantasía presente, y luego
                de allí van a parar dentro al tesoro
                de toda semejanza inteligible...                            15

                                (R, 48)

A comparable passage involving similar terminology occurs in the more expansive *Carta a Galanio* when the poet remembers his friend's letter with its account of unhappy love:

                Entonces la memoria tesorera
                De aquella, y desta material riqueza
                Del angulo interior, donde hospedea
                Las desamadas, y amistadas formas                          65
                Segun la voluntad se las ofrece
                Como tocada fue, como la hiere
                Relampago de luz tan repentino,
                Luego se acuerda de vna vuestra carta
                Galanio que el discurso contenia                           70
                De los amores tragicos que vn tiempo
                Tratastes con Merisa mas amada
                De vos que el coraçon con que la amastes.

                                (OC, I, 200-01)

As these examples reveal, the philosophic component is an obtrusive feature in Aldana's epistles. He does not wear his learning lightly. Although the allusion in the *Carta a Don Bernardino de Mendoza* to «las digresiones / que hago» is false modesty on the poet's part, there is no escaping the fact that at worst the epistles are ponderous and ungainly. This is not merely a matter of prolixity —frequently caused by the multiplication of analogies— but something that can be attributed to a tendency to the long, rambling sentence as, for example, in this passage from the *Carta a Don Bernardino de Mendoza:*

                En fin tan ygualmente esta assentada
                La tierra en medio, que ocasion no tiene
                Para mudar lugar, que si mudase
                Fuerça seria caer, ya que ygualmente

Dista de todo, toda junta en todo:                        60
Y assi en vn mismo instante el mouimiento
Alto, y baxo seria, diestro, y siniestro:
Adelante, y atras, y a la redonda
Cosa que a la razon tan mal consuena:
Por donde se concluye que la tierra                       65
No puede no tener su medio firme.

(OC, I, 115)

In such places, the dual claims of the philosophic and the colloquial collide;
the impression of Horatian urbanity and common sense, present in earlier
Spanish poets, yields to the earnestness of a tract — the philosopher-acade-
mician in full flight. Furthermore, Aldana is not averse on occasion to a
specific acknowledgement of his sources: in the *Carta a Galanio,* eminent
Aristotelians such as Avicenna and Albertus Magnus are cited within the
one section (ll. 108, 127). Aldana also draws on scientific Aristotelianism
to embellish his ideas with analogies. Thus in the *Carta a don Bernardino
de Mendoza* we come across a passage praising the recipient as repository of
virtue, an Aristotelian commonplace that involves the repeated use of the
term «medio» (ll. 10-66). This eulogy is developed via a series of analogies
drawn from astrology, anatomy and astronomy, specifically presented as
indicators of balance and moderation. The following passage, that makes
use of ideas relating to the location and functions of the heart, is characteristic of the poet's intellectualism at its best. It unites anatomical, astronomi-
cal and even legal concepts in a passage that is purposeful yet discursive
enough for an epistle:

Assi en medio del pecho ha colocado                       30
Aquel cuerpo vital, cuya figura
Imita a las Pyramides de Egypto,
Que por su nombre coraçon se llama,
Y en quien assi como en la Esphera octaua
Miramos tanta biua luminaria                              35
De estrellas a la vista plateadas,
Que van con el reglado mouimiento
De quien las lleua dando ley a todo,
Y assi dentro este colocado en medio
Cuerpo Pyramidal como en su centro                        40
Exalan mil espiritus vitales,
Que en circulo despues yendo, y viniendo
Ministran al pulmon, ayre de vida,
Y a las arterias incessable pulso...

(OC, I, 114)

The principal problems confronting Aldana in his three blank-verse epistles are structural ones. His response to this challenge is typically adventurous: indeed he provides three different solutions. In all these poems form
is an important consideration. Thus a quest for continuity, balance and sym-

metry is often uppermost. In none of the three works does Aldana allow the epistolary element to excuse the need for organization and unity.

The *Carta a Don Bernardino de Mendoza,* from which the preceding example was drawn, is one of Aldana's many unfinished compositions. It is noticeable that its final paragraph produces a tailing-off effect rather as in the incomplete *Otavas sobre el bien de la vida retirada* to be considered below. The emotional climax of the poem comes twenty-five lines or so before the end in a passage that is reminiscent of Fray Luis de León —an *a lo divino* version of the Horatian *Beatus ille:*

> O venturoso tu, que alla tan alto
> Por do rompiendo va nuestro nauio,
> Tan lexos deste mar tempestuoso
> Habitas, y por termino, y tan casto
> Tan fuera el corporal vso del hombre,                    160
> Buscas a Dios, y en Dios todo lo cierto.
>
> (OC, I, 119)

Yet despite its unsatisfactory ending the poem possesses, even as it stands, a clear balance and symmetry. The first part (ll. 1-89) — by accident or design almost exactly the first half of the work — expands on the idea of virtue. This grows naturally out of the poet's acknowledgement of Don Bernardino's letter:

> Vuestra carta ley, que escrita vino                    10
> En verso, cuya alegre consonancia
> Està do la virtud reside, y mora.
> Cosa admirable es esta, que aun en cosas
> A vuestro entendimiento tan ligeras
> Como el trato comun de amigas cartas                    15
> Iamas querays dexar lugar alguno
> Do la virtud no este puesta en su medio.
>
> (113)

In conjunction with this there appears the modesty *topos,* incorporated so as to form a continuation of the encomium. This leads to a view of friendship that relates to the Neoplatonic concept of the union of souls:

> Que el quereros mostrar dotrina en versos
> Es dar agua a la mar, y a sus orillas
> Arenas, luz al sol, yerua a los prados,
> Lagrimas al amante, y como dizen                    75
> Aues nocturnas a la docta Atenas,
> O por mejor dezir dar vnidades
> Teniendo la sin fin al mismo numero.
> Mas que se ha de hazer? bien es que salga
> Con vos que soys de mi la mejor parte...                    80
>
> (116)

83

This is an idea that Aldana also presents at the start of the *Carta a Galanio:*

> Es tan verdad Galanio lo que agora
> Recita Aldino en los presentes versos
> Como es verdad que Aldino, y que Galanio
> Dos nombres son, y sola vn alma biue
> En Galanio, y Aldino solamente.　　　　　　　　　5
> Tanto que yo de mi menos certeza
> Tengo, que biuo, y soy, que en mi vos mismo
> Se que biuis, y soys la mejor parte...
>
> (OC, I, 198) [9]

The first half of the *Carta a Don Bernardino de Mendoza* is then essentially Aristotelian-Horatian in inspiration. The Platonic affiliation of the passage just quoted (ll. 72-80), however, serves to prepare for the introduction of a new theme for the second part. In a nutshell what we have is a change of focus from «virtud» with its Aristotelian resonances to «verdad», which is elaborated in accordance with a Christian-Neoplatonist viewpoint. The second half of the poem is more tightly-knit than the first. It begins with the exposition of a common Golden Age idea, that of «engaño», in order to illustrate the notion that truth is not easily discovered. This passage anticipates ideologically and lexically later Golden Age writers:

> Fue la verdad con alas de paloma　　　　　　　　90
> Desdeñando habitar nuestras cabañas,
> Y en su lugar (como despues del dia
> La noche acude) la mentira vino:
> Y porque al mundo vio tan amoroso,
> Y dado a lo exterior, se ornó la infame　　　　　95
> De cabello sutil, dorado, y crespo.
> Tomo los labios del color que muestran
> La purpura, la grana, y los corales,
> Cubriose de oro, y plata en rico traje
> Alcoholó las cejas, y nombrose　　　　　　　　　100
> Verdad, ved que mentira tan notable?
>
> (OC, I, 117) [10]

The poet consequently counsels withdrawal from the world as a solution. In solitude and denial, he suggests, man encounters fulfilment:

> Aqui reciben la desnuda tierra,
> Y el esteril sarmiento por reposo:
> Aqui quieren passar las breues horas
> Deste del alma temporal destierro,

---

[9] This passage is discussed by RUIZ SILVA, *Estudios sobre Francisco de Aldana*, p. 215.

[10] Compare the allegorical passage on Truth and Justice in Quevedo's *El alguacil endemoniado* and, more specifically, the profound understanding of «engaño» in the dramatization of Beauty and Discretion in Calderón's *No hay más fortuna que Dios.*

Y casi inteligencias separadas                                    135
En cualquier cosa minima que sea,
(Si tal hallar se puede en la natura)
Hallan al hazedor, y alli lo alaban...

(118)

An allusion to the «cueva helada y tenebrosa» (1. 141) together with a specific mention of Socrates (1. 144) and a concentration on the sun and its rays lead to a *locus classicus* of Christian Neoplatonism: the ascent from the real to the ideal:

No por parar alli, que no es objeto
Proporcionado al alma cuerpo alguno,
Mas por subir desde aquel sol visible
Al inuisible sol autor del alma.                                  155

(119)

This is immediately followed by the exclamation quoted previously (ll. 156-61) that constitutes the climax of the poem.

Although the two halves of the poem are clearly distinguishable («virtud» and «verdad» respectively) there are connecting threads. Most obvious is the constant allusion to the sun. In the first part it figures in the extended Aristotelian-inspired analogies as a metaphor drawn from the scientific field; in the second part, it becomes potently symbolic of an area of religious experience. There is, also, a less obvious thread that links the two halves. This entails the use of nautical imagery, a favourite source for both classical and Renaissance writers. Towards the end of the first part, Aldana has recourse to two similes to describe the random, haphazard nature of his writing, so unlike that of the recipient, Don Bernardino. The second of these similes is a ship that cannot reach harbour:

O qual nauio que sin tomar el puerto,                             85
Va dando bordos con hinchada vela
Aca, y alla cien mil tomando puntas.

(116)

The poet does not lose sight of this image despite its apparently casual elaboration here. In the section describing the dangers involved in the search for truth, Aldana refers to the pleasures of life metaphorically as «la navegación de aquesta vida» (1. 112). Again, as we have seen, the nautical aspect dominates the poem's climactic exclamation. The solitary, contemplative life, free from the hazards and fatal distractions of the world, is envisaged as an existence «lexos deste mar tempestuoso» (1. 158) where the ship of life founders: «Por do rompiendo va nuestro nauio» (1. 157). This repetition of images lends the poem an air of logical development despite the abrupt thematic shift from «virtud» to «verdad».

The *Carta a Galanio* is by far the longest of the epistles, and includes as an unusual, if not unique feature, a postscript which amounts to a quarter of the whole poem. Of Galanio, nothing is known. [11] He figures as a confidant in *soneto* XVI («Galanio, tú sabrás que esotro día»), but unlike the pseudonyms used in the *Respuesta a Cosme* (Hernadio, Silvio, Arceo) there is no evidence of any real-life identity. The content of the epistle, indeed, might lead us to doubt his existence as a real person. Although Galanio's letter is in the nature of a highly personal account («los amores trágicos que vn tiempo / Tratastes con Merisa»), Aldana's poem lacks that note of friendship and intimacy that might have been expected in the circumstances and which we certainly encounter in the *Respuesta a Cosme*.

The main body of the poem is concerned with love, informed by two perspectives corresponding to the poet and the recipient respectively. The former assumes the role of the experienced, worldly, slightly sceptical adviser who counsels the unfortunate Galanio by a blend of specific observation and more general philosophizing. In this poem the principal philosophic component is amatory.

But while the basic framework of the poem is built on two attitudes, in the postscript these voices merge. The poet, identified by the pseudonym Aldino, opts to speak on behalf of Galanio and addresses Merisa as if she were present. He states that he is prevented by a sudden surge of indignation from bringing the letter to a close:

> Postdata. Yo quisiera mi Galanio
> Enmudecer aqui, trauar la lengua,
> Iunto, papel, memoria, y pluma junto 530
> Sacrificar por siempre al Dios herrero,
> Y assi me leuantè por no escriuiros
> Mas de lo escrito, empero quise apenas
> Esta carta cerrar, quando vn despecho,
> Vn tropel de dolor, vn gran torrente 535
> De colera inflamada me arrebata,
> Y con palabras de silencio triste
> Me dize. Estate aqui. Di lo que digo...
>
> (220)

What follows is a lengthy rebuke of the *amada*. The poet chides her for her cruelty and lack of faith. Words like «cruel», «fiera», «cruda», «perjura», «engañosa», «mentirosa» and «vana» colour the poet's recrimination and he concludes, while still assuming the role of Galanio, that Merisa is unworthy of his affection (ll. 693-94). There follows an indication of jealousy as the poet *vice* Galanio dismisses Merisa. This passage recalls Salicio's jealous reproach in Garcilaso's *Eclogue* I:

[11] ALFREDO LEFEBVRE (*La poesía del capitán Aldana*, p. 49) believes that Galanio could also be the recipient of the *Pocos tercetos* in view of the amatory element common to both poems.

> Sus vete, vete ya, ni mas parezcas
> Ante mis ojos, huye de mi vista 700
> Apartate de mi para en eterno:
> Conversa esse Pastor necio, y siluestre...
>
> (227)

The device adopted in the postscript is such as to lend credence to the idea that Galanio is a fiction and that both he and Aldino are figures of the poet —*personae* who represent differing attitudes towards love, the one involved, the other more detached. Such an interpretation would provide an interesting, more literal, variation of the Neoplatonic commonplace of the union of souls, expressed in the opening lines of the poem (quoted above, p. 84).

The very vehemence of the final section marks it out as that part of the poem where involvement and indignation are most conspicuous. Such an attitude contrasts with the note of respect towards the lady that is normally found in amatory epistles and love-elegies. It is, however, quite in keeping with the trenchant approach to love such as was evident in the previous chapters.

The central section (ll. 256-527) is given over entirely to an examination of love. It comprises an alternation of the general and the specific and the organization is neat and seamless. The section opens with a definition of love of a kind commonly found in Renaissance poetry: love is Cupid —«el Niño Arquero»— a powerful and ingenious figure who provokes both wonder and criticism:

> Ved la sagacidad deste mal niño,
> Ved la simplicidad deste embustero, 265
> Deste que assi dire gitano espiritu.
> En fin yo dixe, y digo, y dire siempre
> Que Amor es vna lucha no entendida
> De mil traspies, enredos, y marañas,
> Vn terrible sophista que argumenta 270
> Con la misma verdad muy sin verguença.
>
> (209)

There then follows a passage in which the poet moves to the specific and refers to letters written by Merisa to Galanio at the time when she was in love with him. Turning again to Galanio's letter, the poet singles out his sadness at not seeing Merisa and from this constructs a meditation on absence in love, exploring very theoretically the common metaphor of absence as a death. This passage is perhaps over-long not least because what Aldana is doing is to engender philosophic depth from a commonplace. None-the-less, the occasional observation reveals an eye for original, thought-provoking rationalization, as when the poet suggests that the fear of death is a consequence of a prior experience of absence —effectively a reversal of the metaphor:

87

Y tengo por muy cierto que la pena
Causada del morir nace de solo
Parecerse a la ausencia dura, y triste.                      343

(212)

Characteristic too of Aldana at his best is the climax of this passage: an
exclamation in the form of an address to absence. The imagery is vivid and
the recourse to alliteration to highlight the contrast of «altura» and «abismo» is a sensitive touch:

Ay fiera ausencia que en las altas cumbres
Biues, de soledad mirando el valle,
Por do las aguas corren del oluido,
Y desde aquella altura aquel abismo
Despeñas las memorias amorosas.                      360

(213)

In the next sub-section, which returns to the specific relationship, there
is perhaps a further hint that Galanio and Aldino are one and the same.
Firstly there appears a short passage in which the poet puts words into
Galanio's mouth on the pretext of wondering whether he had, in fact,
expressed such sentiments (ll. 386-95). This is followed by an admission
by Aldino that he too once experienced the bitterness of love, although he
is now free of its shackles:

Que me dezis Galanio, es algo desto,
Lo que dexistes vos? mas quien lo duda?
Tambien yo nauegue por essos mares,
Tambien yo fuy soldado en essa guerra,
Y el tributo pague de aquellos años                      400
Que al niño arquero son mas agradables.
Mas ya podre dezir passò solia,
Que el Ebano del pelo ya blanquea.

(214)

The amatory content of the poem could then be defined as a contrast between past indulgence in love and present freedom from it —a common
enough antithesis in the love poetry of this period. [12] Such a definition would
be consistent with the interpretation of the poem as the enunciation of two
perspectives by the one person rather than as an exchange between two
separate figures.

The principal section of the poem concludes with a discussion about
different kinds of love. This arises from a specific allusion in Galanio's

---

[12] For an examination of the varied responses of such poets as Herrera, Lope de
Vega, Lupercio Leonardo de Argensola and Quevedo to the theme of past love see
the reference in Chapter 3, note 13.

letter to the union of souls. It provokes a scathing and ironic response in the poet as he mentions Plato's Androgyne myth:

> Donosa conversion de dos que buscan 430
> Los cuerpos conuertir como las Almas,
> Vno en otro, y ser nueuo Androgino.
>
> (216)

He mocks the notion that such a fusion could be founded on physical love, and, warming to his subject, draws a distinction between human («mundano») and divine love. The one may reflect the other but in no sense are they interchangeable:

> No es essa conuersion por Dios traçada,
> Mas vn estremo, oppuesto al conuertirse,
> No por que el yelo queme a la verdura. 435
> Y la pueda quemar tambien el fuego
> Por esso el yelo es fuego, el fuego es yelo.
> No por que vos llegarades al punto
> De efectuar lo mismo, que pensastes
> Fuera Diuino Amor la causa dello, 440
> Mas su contrario del que es el mundano,
> Y dado que a esse Amor, y a esse otro llamen
> Tambien Amor, sabras que para siempre
> Son, y seran Amores paralelos,
> Que no pueden juntarse a ningun termino. 445
>
> (216) [13]

Structurally the poem fails because of its prolixity. Nowhere is this more evident than in the opening section. It occupies more than a third of the entire composition and yet contains little by way of thematic substance nor has it any connection with what is to follow. The Aristotelian-inspired realization of the workings of the imagination and memory is a sprawling passage that eventually leads to a celebrated section (ll. 150-246) comprising a detailed description of a military camp at night in a state of sudden alarm, including a vivid picture of an agitated horse. This passage has appeared in at least one anthology as an independent piece. [14] Yet, in context, it is only an analogy within the preamble to the poem. It illustrates the effect of grief on the poet's heart, causing his body to swoon until, with a sigh, he returns to his normal state:

---

[13] This passage is briefly commented on by OTIS H. GREEN in his chapter «Courtly Love and Platonic Vision», in *Spain and the Western Tradition. The Castilian Mind in Literature from* El Cid *to Calderón,* vol. I (Madison, Milwaukee and London: University of Wisconsin Press, 1968), p. 123.

[14] In *The Penguin Book of Spanish Verse,* ed. J. M. COHEN (Harmondsworth: Penguin Books, 1960), pp. 177-78.

De esta manera, que aqui pinto agora  
Las potencias del alma, y las corporeas  
Reñidas reboltosas, y açoradas.  
Senti Galanio en mi pequeño Mundo.                                    250  
Mas buelta como he dicho toda cosa  
A su lugar, tambien la mente clara  
A Galanio beluió, que es lugar suyo.  
A ponderar comiença muy despacio  
Mi porcion superior vuestros successos.                              255

(208)

Self-indulgent though the *Carta a Galanio* is, passages such as these reveal a talent willing to embrace the broad vision; it is the product of a poetic outlook and ambitiousness that could envisage an artefact like the *Carta para Arias Montano*. [15]

The *Respuesta a Cosme* is perhaps the best integrated of all Aldana's verse epistles. It was written in Flanders in 1568 in response to a letter that has survived from Cosme. [16] Fraternal affection also inspired Francisco to write a sonnet («Cual sin arrimo vid, cual planta umbrosa») on his feelings of dejection at being away from Cosme. Something of the structural rigour of this *soneto* XXVI (an extended anaphora) is apparent in the verse epistle, although there is no evidence as to which was the earlier composition. In various places in the *Respuesta a Cosme* we catch a glimpse of the poet subjecting himself to restraint and discipline. At regular intervals in the second part of the poem he refers to his good state of health. [17] The repetition of such a casual observation —apt enough in itself for a familiar letter— acquires the function of a motif, serving to mark boundaries and to curtail discursiveness. Thus an allusion to the poet's health in ll. 103-05 separates the section on the loss of inspiration from that on conditions in Flanders. An even briefer mention in ll. 148-49 serves as a transition between the latter section and one in which he pays tribute to his mother.

But such practices serve thematic purposes too. The idea of «salud» is not only a convenient marker of sections; in its final appearance it merges with the concept, present in other verse epistles, of the union of the writer and the recipient: «porque mi salud vive en la vuestra» (R, 54; 1. 180).

---

[15] As with the extended description in the *Carta a Galanio* so too in the *Carta para Arias Montano* Aldana envisages the climactic set-piece description —that of the sea-shore— in terms of painting: «quiero el lugar pintar» (1. 353).

[16] This letter is printed in OC, I, 122-30 and in *Epistolario poético completo*, pp. 32-38.

[17] This idea may reveal the influence of GARCILASO's *Epístola a Boscán*:

y así, d'aquesta libertad gozando,  
digo que vine, cuanto a lo primero,  
tan sano como aquel que en doce días  
lo que sólo veréis ha caminado  
cuando el fin de la carta os lo mostrare.

(*Ed. cit.*, p. 116)

This accounts for the poet's well-being in an alien, inhospitable environment; by means of the friendship *topos* the concept of «salud» is raised from a physical to a spiritual condition. This interpretation is clearly confirmed by the words Aldana puts into the mouth of his mother when he imagines her praying for him:

> «¡Hijo eterno de Dios, pues que Tú eres
> salud universal, camino y vida
> de nuestra salvación, salva y conserva
> en próspera salud a mi Francisco!»                165
>
> (R, 54)

Here Aldana plays on the two meanings of «salud» —health and salvation.[18]

This is but one instance, although perhaps the most subtle, of the poem's coherence. Much use is made of antithesis. We have already seen the contrast between a present loss of inspiration and former creative prowess. To this contrast is attached one of place. The poet nostalgically recalls the Florentine setting as a lost paradise, an idyllic location, described in pastoral terms:

> Y bien me acuerdo yo que allá en el monte
> y allá en el valle, a la ribera de Arno
> (¡ay monte, ay valle, ay Arno, ay mi Ribera;
> cómo vivo yo aquí lloroso y triste!)...                84
>
> (R, 51)

Against this «dorado y claro día» is set «la tenebrosa noche» (ll. 91-92) of Flanders —a night that is envisaged literally as well as metaphorically in a passage that describes the horrors of the Northern European winter for the southerner:

> Ni me quiero alargar, Cosme süave,
> a describir esta región do vivo,
> do en un cerco solar de un año entero,
> menos tan sólo un mes, yo nunca he visto
> la serena del sol cara sin nube.                135
> Y si por suerte el velo húmido y negro
> de sus ventanas abre algún resquicio
> por do un rayo de luz se muestre al suelo,
> en pago de merced tan transitoria
> vuelve a cerrarse y con vapor más grueso                140

---

[18] A similar pun is to be found at the end of Petrarch's sonnet «Or che 'l ciel e la terra e 'l vento tace» (*Canzoniere*, CLXIV):

> E perche 'l mio martìr non giunga a riva
> mille volte il dì moro e mille nasco;
> tanto da la salute mia son lunge.

nos carga de manera que al sol mismo
llega la opacidad que sube en alto
sin que la luz de allá se lo defienda.

(R, 53)

The concept of darkness is also employed in connection with a vague allusion to strife and intrigue at the Spanish court in Brussels («este abismo
y centro / oscuro de mentira») — a passage slightly marred by excessive
punning:

La vida que ora paso aquí no es otra
que trafagar en esta corte ibera.                                    115
¿No veis, ¡válgame Dios!, cuán cortamente
os vengo yo a decir que estoy en corte,
como si fuese alguna cosa corta
para poder meterse en breve carta?
No quiero entrar en este abismo y centro                             120
oscuro de mentira, en esta inmensa
de torpe vanidad circunferencia,
que nunca acabaría...

(R, 52)

How different to the Arcadian scene on the banks of the Arno with his
friends: «mi Hernadio», «mi Cosme», «mi Silvio» and «mi Arceo» (ll.
85-87).

Another indication of how tautly organized is the *Respuesta a Cosme*
comes in a brief tribute to the Duke of Alba, who is addressed as «señor y
amigo» (1. 106). In these few lines of conventional encomium, reminiscent
of the dedicatory element in pastoral and epic poetry, the two aspects of
friendship and tribute neatly encapsulate the two attitudes revealed in the
poem towards the brother and the mother respectively. One can also note
a connection between the notion of the poet acquiring immortality through
association with the Duke:

oh cómo pienso, oh cómo, inmortalarme
con el nombre inmortal deste gran hombre!                            113

(R, 52)

and the description of his mother as his source of life:

aquella santa, aquella casta y pura
lengua de mi piadosa engendradora...                                152

(R, 54)

The *Respuesta a Cosme* is the lightest and yet most structurally complex
of the verse epistles, and is perhaps the most appealing of these poems. It
epitomizes Renaissance humanism in its spiritual though not predominantly

other-worldly orientation and in its celebration of human relationships. While in this latter respect it recalls the essays of Cicero on friendship, in its tone —specifically in the subordination of the philosophical to the particular— it recaptures the urbanity of Horace's *Epistles* and *Satires*. But its blend of informality and structural awareness marks it out as a poem *sui generis,* a significant development of the manner adopted in Garcilaso's pioneering *Epístola a Boscán* and yet free of the overt moralizing of other Golden Age verse epistles.

# 6

## POLITICAL AND RELIGIOUS POETRY: THE PUBLIC VOICE

For most of his adult life Aldana was involved in some form or other in military affairs. He was initiated into battle at an early age: in a memorandum written towards the end of his life he infers that he was a soldier by 1553, his sixteenth year. [1] In 1557 he participated in the Battle of St Quentin and in 1563 became a lieutenant to his father on the latter's appointment as governor of the fortress of San Miniato. His principal campaign was in the Low Countries between 1567 and 1576, and prior to his death in the disaster of Alcazarquivir in 1578 he had been engaged in a more diplomatic or advisory capacity, including, for a short period, the post of governor of the fortress of San Sebastián.

As with Garcilaso, Aldana's public life seldom intrudes upon his literary enterprises; like Luis de León, his poetry responds, implicitly and sometimes explicitly, to a desire for withdrawal, privacy and self-communion. But given the background of a quarter of a century's involvement in some of the important events affecting the Iberian Peninsula in a period of fluctuating fortunes, it is only to be expected that Aldana should on occasion have focussed his attention on the political and military affairs of his day. Nonetheless his written observations on such matters are few; even among the lost works there is no evidence from the titles or descriptions of works of material either in verse or prose on such issues, unless it is among the missing letters to which Cosme draws attention. [2] Aldana's political poetry, in fact, forms a smaller group than his religious verse. Furthermore, the political is unmistakably permeated by the religious as befits the sixteenth-century Spaniard's view of the world. Only occasionally is the voice of the soldier,

---

[1] In a letter to Philip II dated 15 September 1577 in which he reviews his military career in the King's service, Aldana states that he had served him for twenty-four years. Archivo General de Simancas. Guerra Antigua, leg. 82, fol. 156. See RUIZ SILVA, *Estudios sobre Francisco de Aldana*, pp. 23-24.

[2] To judge by Cosme's description, his brother's letters seem even more varied in mood than his epistolary verse: «[Faltan] muchas cartas muy doctas sobre varios sujetos, y otras ridiculas, y llenas de gracia, donayres, burlas, y buenos dichos» (OC, II, 255).

purely and simply, heard, as in the following stanza from the *Otavas dirigidas al rey don Felipe, Nuestro Señor:*

> Hacer seis cosas pueden resistencia 225
> a toda mano armada que guerrea:
> soldados con calezas de esperiencia,
> plaza, foso y través que fuerte sea,
> dificultad de sitio, en eminencia
> do la misma natura es quien pelea; 230
> y faltan todas seis por el costado
> de España que debiera ser guardado.
>
> (R, 109)

These lines are informed by experience and know-how —the words of one who understands his craft. Similarly authentic is the long section in the *Carta a Galanio* in which there is a description of an alarm in a military camp at night. This is a particularly detailed and evocative passage that contains an extended use of violent *enjambement:*

> Luego vereys la boz multiplicada
> Difusa, y repetida en toda boca,
> Hazia el primer rumor ya corren todos,
> Las sonorosas caxas ya retumban,
> Aquel toma el escudo, este, el estoque. 185
> Este, y aquel la lança, otro la pica,
> Otro la espada, esse otro el instrumento,
> Que relampago, rayo, y trueno junto
> Echa de si con daño de mil vidas
> Aquel su cuerda enciende, este su mecha 190
> Sopla. De balas este boca, y bolsa
> Hinche. Quien la trauada y vieja malla
> Cubre. Quien la manopla, y la celada
> Toma...
>
> (OC, I, 205-06) [3]

But the vision in the few poems in which Aldana comments on national matters is generally broad and sweeping. Furthermore, while his view of military life is complex, not to say ambivalent, no such uncertainties affect his assessment of Spain's place in the world and her particular destiny. The tone is ringing and confident; a modern sensibility may find it shrill and arrogant:

> Desde la eternidad, antes que el cielo
> amaneciese al mundo el primer día,
> nombrado, oh gran Felipe, Dios te había
> por rey universal de todo el suelo;

---

[3] This passage is discussed by RUIZ SILVA, *Estudios sobre Francisco de Aldana,* pp. 198-99.

y así como esparció con tanto celo
Bautista la venida del Mesía,
así ora Juan de un polo al otro envía,
tras su fama inmortal, tu cetro a vuelo.
  Ha seis mil años casi que camina
el mundo con el tiempo a consagrarte
la grey diversa reducida en una:
  ¡oh cómo en ti paró la edad más dina
bien dinamente, y va tras tu estandarte
la gente, el mundo, el tiempo y la fortuna.

(R, 20)

This Messianic utterance —Aldana's *soneto* XXVII— follows very much in the footsteps of another sonnet to Philip II, written a number of years earlier by Hernando de Acuña. For example, the «grey diversa reducida en una» of Aldana's poem recalls Acuña's reference to «la edad gloriosa, en que promete el cielo / una grey, y un pastor, solo en el suelo»,[4] while both sonnets partake of the same military iconography: the vision of the peoples of the world united under the one banner. In Acuña's poem, Philip has been granted Christ's standard and spiritual uniformity and military conquest march hand in hand:

  que, a quien ha dado Cristo su estandarte,
  dará el segundo más dichoso día
  en que, vencido el mar, venza la tierra.

It is easy to underrate such poetry especially if we allow an antipathy to the subject-matter to over-rule an assessment of the poem's more immediate, if limited, poetic import. Aldana's sonnet is not great poetry, nor even his best, but it has a deft craftsmanship about it. For example, the identification of John of Austria with John the Baptist, preparing the way for the Messiah, is neatly realized, though perhaps the more impressive aspects of the poem are its stylistic touches, in particular those brought about by a restrained but telling use of hyperbaton. The separation of the past participle «nombrado» from its auxiliary in line 3 creates an appropriately weighty and dignified tripartite line, and by displacing the participle to the start of the line an emphasis is given to the idea of destiny. In the second quatrain the inversion of the verb («esparció») enables the poet to compose a ringingly assonantal sixth line («Bautista la venida del Mesía») — again creating intensity at an apt moment. The tercets are less impressive. The repetition («dina», «dinamente») adds nothing, while the enumeration of the last line does not carry as much weight as the poet might have hoped perhaps because of a semantic weakness: the succession of nouns does not provide a sense of

---

 [4] I quote from *Varias poesías*, ed. Luis F. Díaz Larios (Madrid: Cátedra, 1982), pp. 328-29.

progression or *crescendo* such as we find, for example, at the conclusion of some of Góngora's sonnets when a similar technique is employed. [5]

The sonnet alludes to the extent of Spain's empire and to its global ambitions; the news of Don John of Austria's victory at Lepanto heralds even greater exploits. The notion of Spain's vast territories is the key idea of a sonnet dedicated to Philip II's fourth wife, Anne of Austria, whom he married in 1570:

> Puso el Señor del cielo en vuestra cara
> tanto de lo admirable y peregrino,
> que el mundo fuera acá de vos indino
> si por señora dél Dios no os crïara.
> En veros, la razón distinta y clara
> se ve, que fué decreto alto y divino
> reina ser vos del Ártico al Austrino
> y mucho más, si el Sol más rodeara.
> Nunca llegó deseo ni pensamiento
> a descubrir de vista el bien que agora,
> Ana real, goza por vos el suelo:
> tanto que el estrellado firmamento
> al suelo invidia, y más querría la Aurora
> ser vuestra luz que del que alumbra el cielo.
>
> (R, 21)

For his eulogy, Aldana combines the idea of the immense empire with a standard mode of praising female beauty; the result is an interesting brand of political Petrarchism. [6] Aldana departs from the Messianic idea («decreto alto y divino») that Anne is destined to be queen over lands from the Arctic to the Antarctic, and expands on this hyperbolically in the manner of a love poet extravagantly praising his mistress. Thus she would be queen of even more lands if only the sun could increase its orbit (clearly the standpoint is pre-Copernican!); such is her beauty that the world would be unworthy of her if she had not been destined to rule over it as queen; the starry sky envies the earth for having a greater sun in its midst, and dawn would prefer to be produced by the lady's light than by the sun. These are standard compliments but the combination and development here of two different modes (the heroic and the amatory) produce a poem that is neither as slight nor as pompous as some examples of the genre.

---

[5] The most notable example is the last line of the *carpe diem* sonnet «Mientras por competir con tu cabello»: «en tierra, en humo, en polvo, en sombra, en nada» (*ed. cit.,* p. 230).

[6] At the same time in England, the Petrarchist image of the ideal lady was being assiduously cultivated by Elizabeth I. It was not «merely a convenient device to enable courtiers to turn graceful compliments. It had practical political importance: it enabled the Queen to hold powerful and dangerous suitors or potential rivals at arm's length while keeping them on a string. It seems likely that she adopted it and maintained it of set purpose». FORSTER, *The Icy Fire,* p. 127.

Female protagonists play a role too in Aldana's longest and most ambitious political poem, the *Otavas dirigidas al rey don Felipe*. The two women referred to at the outset of the poem are personifications of the Church and the Military. Why Aldana should have chosen such a method of description is not altogether clear unless it be on account of a passing allusion to the symbolism of the Church as the bride of Christ in stanza 6 and an application of this symbol to the other figure in the allegory. But there is some development of this feminine aspect in an occasionally surprising fashion. There is much delicacy in the description of the woman who represents the Church («altivamente humilde y reposado»):

> suelto el cabello en nazarena y breve
> forma, y de lirios frescos el tocado,
> tan casta, tan gentil, graciosa y bella,                       15
> que el aire en torno se enamora della.
>
> (R, 102)

The final line recalls the ethereal opening of Luis de León's *Oda a Francisco de Salinas:* «El aire se serena / y viste de hermosura y luz no usada». But such moments are rare in this poem and the key to its martial, even fanatical, tone is to be found in the ninth stanza:

> ¿Ya ves con cuánta gracia junta y cierra              65
> sus manos de alabastro y pone en alto?
> Pues manos son también que a dura guerra
> Dios enseñó y a belicoso asalto,
> cuyo valor con sólo un dedo atierra
> al Centro el ángel tenebroso y falto               70
> y, con ser dedo, el brazo al mundo liga
> y a la mayor doméstica enemiga.
>
> (103)

The gentle femininity portrayed in the first two lines is brusquely swept aside by the evocation of warfare and the sound of battle. Indeed for the remainder of the poem the reader is apt to forget the significance of the personification as what could be termed its standard associations are negated. For example, in these lines the reference to the sadness experienced by the Church is consolidated by a couple of lines of sweet delicacy:

> Muévate, ¡oh rey!, el tierno y largo lloro
> desta Esposa gentil que ves presente;             690
> mira ondear al aire el sotil oro;
> mira el sereno cielo de esa frente...
>
> (126)

But about fifty lines below such tears are seen metaphorically in a strikingly different light:

Las lágrimas que ves tan abundantes,
que el dulce rostro de la Esposa riegan,
son sus validas armas militantes
que, sembradas en tierra, al Cielo llegan...          740

(127)

It is only in the final stanza that Aldana, as a last gesture, reintroduces unambiguously the full significance of the feminine allegory when the two women take leave of the King, and the Church is described in these terms:

ella también, cual matutina estrella,
su rostro vuelto al rey claro y ardiente,
háblóle con los ojos de manera
que al más helado risco enterneciera.          880

(132)

The poem itself offers both a diagnosis of and a remedy for the political reality of Spain in the 1570s. Its concern is with the dangers confronting the nation at a number of pressure points; the remedy is action, and sooner rather than later:

¡Venga el brazo español, venga la hacha;
córtese deste tronco vida y nombre,
deste que ver al sol la vista empacha,
antes que su gran sombra nos asombre!          300
Dar tiempo al tiempo es perjüicio y tacha
cuando con tiempo puede obrar el hombre,
pues suelen, de provechos o de daños,
en un momento consistir mil años.

(112)

Aldana urges a mood of exultant patriotism:

despierte la española lozanía,
que nunca tuvo la marcial fiereza
enemigo mayor que la tristeza.          328

(112)

The call for prompt and decisive action is repeated several times in the course of the poem. A favoured metaphor is taken from agriculture:

Mas quiero dar que agora nadie venga          385
en daño de tu rica y fertil miese:
¿qué te puede dañar que se prevenga
a la necesidad, cuando viniese?
El cauto labrador, para que tenga
del campesino afán rico interese,          390
lanza de sí la rica simentera
para la estéril hambre venidera.

(115)

> Duerme el agricultor, duerme, y el trigo
> confunde y mezcla de dañosa avena
> el sin piedad, solícito enemigo,
> gozoso de su culpa y de su pena...                    764
>
> (128)

As can be judged from the few examples already quoted, the poem is characterized by an extreme nationalism, expressed in a language that is lurid and inflammatory. It is a distillation of what are for many the worst qualities of Spain's Golden Age: intolerance, xenophobia, self-satisfaction and suspicion. Ruiz Silva indeed is of the opinion that one of the stanzas in the poem should appear in an anthology of «la brutalidad e intransigencia ibérica».[7] As a consequence the poem is interesting, even fascinating, from a historian's angle. No other work of this period communicates as vividly the experience of a nation, at once dominant and threatened. It expresses the acute sense of insecurity only a few years after the triumph at Lepanto and reveals how short-lived and deceptive the euphoria surrounding that event was. The emotional keynote of the poem is fear: Spain is a country under siege, menaced on all sides and especially from Africa:

> tan cerca está de nuestro ibero asiento          245
> África, por el mar que nos rodea,
> que puede cuanto tiene en sí de bueno
> de presto trasladarlo al patrio seno.
>
> (110)

The old enemy, the Moor, is a constant threat. Not even the inhospitable Iberian terrain deters him, as history should have taught:

> Es voz común de la vulgar rudeza
> que la falta de humor que España tiene,
> y sobra de desierto y de aspereza,                    235
> lo hace defensión contra el que viene;
> y no sabe entender con qué estrecheza
> de nutrimento el moro se mantiene,
> como en el siglo atrás bien claro vimos
> cuando el paterno límite perdimos.                    240
>
> (109)

Aldana casts his glance back over the centuries to the emotive event of 711 when the last Visigothic king, Rodrigo, was defeated by a Moorish army. The poet claims that Spain is even more perilously placed at the time he writes, beset as it is by enemies on all sides and by a threat within —the Moriscos. The final allusion in this stanza is to the rebellion of the Alpujarras in the late 1560s:

---

[7] *Estudios sobre Francisco de Aldana*, p. 191.

> Cuatro en nuestro favor cosas había
> en aquel siglo, en esto venturoso:
> que el scítico Mahoma no corría             195
> sobre el cristiano mar tan poderoso,
> ni el gálico poder le recogía,
> ni el fementido hereje caviloso
> armaba el pecho, ni en el pueblo insano
> había la rebelión puesto la mano.          200
>
> (108)

The remedy, or rather the instinctive reaction, is the need for breathing-space, a kind of *Lebensraum*. The enemy is best kept at a safe distance:

> No venga a avecindar, de España en frente,
> nueva Constantinopla poderosa,
> que cuanto más cercana y más potente,      275
> tanto será más grave y más dañosa.
> No beba el scita el agua de tu fuente;
> navegue allá tu flota numerosa;
> no tengamos gigantes por vecinos,
> que es casi contrastar con los destinos.     280
>
> (111)

The point is reinforced by a Biblical analogy, a procedure that Aldana adopts increasingly towards the end of the poem as it becomes more diffuse and digressive:

> David, que vió tan grande al filisteo,
> no se juntó con él, mas, advertido,
> de lejos le tiró, y así el trofeo
> quedó por suyo, y fué el jayán vencido...     284
>
> (111)

To condemn the *Otavas dirigidas al rey don Felipe* for its bigotry and excessive nationalism is not so much a reflection on the poetic value of the work itself as on the socio-historical circumstances in which it was composed. The stridency and obsessiveness are admittedly inhibiting and unattractive features and Ruiz Silva's strictures are understandable if not altogether justifiable as an assessment of the poem as work of art. But I believe that the piece can be faulted as much for its realization as for its concept and content.

I have already drawn attention to the incongruity of the female personifications and the descriptions that derive from them. Moreover, the figurative devices employed in this connection —metaphors and similes drawn from standard Petrarchism— are not worked with any vigour or originality, unlike the political Petrarchism of the sonnet to Anne of Austria. Such writing is, unfortunately, characteristic of the figurative and decorative processes of the poem as a whole. Biblical and classical analogies are used

101

profusely and indiscriminately, less to illuminate than to browbeat, as in the following *octava* that expands upon the idea of heresy:

> Hacen los filisteos su junta y liga
> contra Sansón, contra el real profeta
> Saúl; contra Moisés se aprieta y liga
> de Datán y Abirón la impura seta;               620
> la gente a Cristo incrédula enemiga
> de su carne especial, santa y perfeta
> no dividieron miembro, y sólo ha sido
> agora en cien mil partes dividido.

(123)

A feature of this *octava* too is its infelicitous combination of a prosaic turn of phrase with metrical awkwardness, seen principally in the first three lines, and exacerbated by a weak rhyme between lines one and three. The ponderous effect of analogy by enumeration and definition contrasts with the lighter but more suggestive utilization of Biblical allusion in another political poem of the period, Herrera's *Canción* on the defeat of the Portuguese army at Alcazarquivir. [8]

Equally weak and ineffective is the following stanza which constitutes part of a passage in which Philip is seen as the sun of all Christians and exhorted to allow his light to shine to the full. Aldana makes heavy weather of this straightforward comparison: the analogy is laboured and introduced by a quite unnecessary circumlocution:

> Contempla el celestial ojo sereno
> que llaman sol, cuál va corriendo suelto     810
> por el alto de allá luciente seno,
> cuán presto a todo el orbe da la vuelta
> y deja verde y fértil el terreno
> con sola su presencia desenvuelta,
> que a no gozar el mundo de su día,          815
> mortal enfermedad padecería...

(130)

Typical of the heavy-handed manner of this poem is the clumsy use of hyperbaton in a passage such as the following:

> los escabrosos riscos no crecieron
> en tu pecho real con su dureza            710
> para que no te mueva esta llorosa,
> que en tu presencia está, de Cristo Esposa...

(126)

---

[8] Details of Old Testament allusions in this poem are to be found in *An Anthology of Spanish Poetry*, ed. ARTHUR TERRY, p. 159.

In short, while the subject of the poem arouses Aldana's concern and indignation, it fails self-evidently to move him to anything remotely like his best as a poet.

Aldana's religious poetry forms a sizeable part of his output but those poems that respond to a more doctrinal or conventional vein do not require as much comment as the more personal utterances concerned with the poet's spiritual experiences. These will occupy my attention in the following, final, chapter.

A handful of Aldana's religious poems are concentrated on the figure of the Virgin, ranging from his longest religious poem, the incomplete *Parto de la Virgen*, based on Sannazzaro's *De Partu Virginis*, to the *canción*, *A la soledad de Nuestra Señora* and to a couple of sonnets. Nothing poetically novel or memorable emerges from these poems although interestingly they are, if anything, more rigorously theological than poems to the Virgin by such notable Biblical scholars as Fray Luis de León and Arias Montano. Aldana, in particular, explores more profoundly and intellectually than his distinguished contemporaries the traditional Roman Catholic view of Mary as the woman figure clothed in the sun —a symbol deriving from Apocalypse 12:1.[9] His Marian poems are characterized by a more mysteriously abstract manner than Fray Luis's *A Nuestra Señora* or Arias Montano's *De la hermosura exterior de Nuestra Señora*, the latter, in fact, being an example of Petrarchism *a lo divino,* as shown in the following lines:

> Rubios son, como el oro
> que en el crisol se acendra, sus cabellos;
> en ellos mi tesoro
> tengo, pues son tan bellos
> que me tiene cautivo en uno dellos.[10]

Aldana does not indulge in such a mode of description. The openings of his two sonnets to the Virgin illustrate his more theologically abstract approach:

> ¡Oh del inmenso Ser concebidora!,
> después de quien sois vos la más subida,
> antes del tiempo amada y conocida
> de la Mente inmortal que os enamora...
>
> (R, 28)

> Hermosa más que el sol, antes nacida
> que el sol, y al ántes mismo delantera,
> pues madre fuiste antes que el tiempo fuera
> del que a los tiempos dió principio y vida...
>
> (R, 29)

[9] See SALSTAD, «Francisco de Aldana's Metamorphoses of the Circle», p. 602.
[10] *Fray Luis de León y la escuela salmantina,* p. 145.

It is the *mater dolorosa* figure that he writes about in the sparse *canción, A la soledad de Nuestra Señora*. It is an accomplished rather than inspired piece; at times, the intensity of the grief is lessened by the use of a phraseology reminiscent of pastoral poetry:

> El sol se asconde de tan gran crüeza,
> la tierra tiembla, el mar combate al cielo,
> y en el gran templo el velo es ya rompido;
> las piedras enternecen su dureza
> y la Natura atemoriza al suelo...                    65
>
> (R, 39)

The Orphean overtones of the last two lines detract somewhat from the impression of turmoil and chaos caused by Christ's death. Moreover, lines like the following are wistful rather than sorrowful, as a result of their secular and mythological connotations, suggestive, for example, of the tale of Persephone:

> El cielo, el suelo y todas las criaturas
> muestran tristeza en vuestra despedida;
> el hombre sólo viste de alegría.                    93
>
> (R, 40)

Nowhere is the lament raised to a higher level, unlike, say, the last stanza of San Juan de la Cruz's sacred parody, *El pastorcico*.

The *Parto de la Virgen* is technically an uneven work; again Aldana eschews the mellifluous or sensuous religiosity of a number of his contemporaries, and it is «la excelencia desta Virgen bella» (OC, II, 41) —a protagonist in the mystery of the Incarnation rather than as a figure susceptible to quasi-pictorial representation— that claims his attention. Even in its unfinished state, the work is a shade over-long and reveals some of Aldana's characteristic weaknesses: the tendency to enumeration, as in the passage describing the journey of the Angel of the Annunciation, and excesses in antithesis and polyptoton, as the following lines reveal:

> O Reyna, pues tu altissima baxeza
> Detuuo en lo mas baxo al Rey mas alto,
> Mi baxa lira sube a tanta alteza,                    195
> Que todo ver mortal me embidie el salto...
>
> (46)

Against this has to be set the artistry of such passages as the one that describes the Angel of the Annunciation before God prior to his mission:

> Cubierto parecio todo de estrellas,
> El moço embazador, ledo, y constante,
> En cuyas alas de oro mil centellas                    315
> Se veen resplandecer casi en Diamante:

Ellas tomando del, y el dando en ellas
Relampago de luz todo ilustrante,
Lleno de Magestad, pero de modo
Que la mesma humildad parece en todo.                    320

(51)

This description is notable for its vivid characterization: both the physical presence of the Angel —the iridescence of his garb— and the spiritual aspect as shown in his demeanour —majestic yet humble— are finely realized.

A highly developed sense of visual representation also informs one of Aldana's doctrinal poems, the *Otavas sobre el Juicio Final*. The visionary aspect is made more immediate by the poet's intrusion in the work as a witness:

Un cerco de oro, al cielo muy vecino,
se descubre a mi ver, nuevo y luciente...

(R, 135)

Jacintos, esmeraldas y diamantes
las nubes se me antoja que pasean
acá y allá con hielos tremolantes,
do varios resplandores centellean,                       20
y en forma de pacíficos amantes
se juntan, se penetran y rodean,
un círculo formando con sus montes,
del cielo por los altos horizontes.

(136)

In this latter quotation, Aldana communicates sensitively a feeling of movement and the momentous; the technique of enumeration, a device he occasionally falls back on too readily, is used to telling effect here, suggesting initially the colour and texture of the clouds («Jacintos, esmeraldas y diamantes») and later their varied movements («se juntan, se penetran y rodean»). It is indeed a pity that not more of this poem has survived for it has much to commend it. The descriptions of the dead as they prepare for judgement reveal a verve and an eye for detail that anticipate Quevedo's account of the Day of Judgement in *El sueño del Juicio Final*:

Quién de sí mismo huye, y quién se toca,
juntando a la atención el movimiento;
otro prueba con voz trémula y loca
de articular el no venido acento.                        100
Éste mueve la lengua, éste la boca;
quién teme de atraer su mismo aliento;
y mientras uno se reforma y cuaja,
otro saltando va con su mortaja.

(138-39)

The following lines reveal perhaps a direct influence of pictorial represen-
tations of hell; they are conceived in the tradition of the Medieval *Danse
macabre,* while their realization recalls the paintings of Bosch and Brueghel:

> ¡Válasme Dios, y cómo veo la muerte
> con podadora hoz cortar mil vidas,           130
> y la vida tornar más firme y fuerte
> a meterse de muerte en las heridas!
> ¡Oh caso nuevo, oh desusada suerte,
> qué de legiones veo de las perdidas,
> porque salen sin cuenta y sin guarismo     135
> millares de demonios del abismo!

(139-40)

It is tempting to relate Aldana's penchant for visual detail in his religious poetry to the *Spiritual Exercises* of St Ignatius Loyola. Indeed, Rivers has shown how one of the poet's non-religious sonnets («Otro aquí no
se ve que, frente a frente») has the hallmarks of the Ignatian scheme of meditation, particularly in the matter of the application of the five senses —a
process that is a conspicuous feature of the *Exercises.* [11] But as R. O. Jones
has warned, perhaps critics have been too eager to ascribe a highly-developed
visual awareness in literature of the late sixteenth and early seventeenth
centuries to the Ignatian scheme. [12] Such a cautionary note is, I feel, appropriate in the case of Aldana. No religious work of his presents as full a
version of the Ignatian meditative process as the *soneto* XXX, although at
least two of his poems, concerned with scenes from the life of Christ, do
suggest the initial stage of the exercise: the *compositio loci.* In both cases,
the poem begins with an indication of place. In a sonnet that deals with
the entombment of Christ, a visual understanding of the scene is specifically
mentioned:

> Yace en esta que veis cava cubierta
> un cuerpo de valor tan soberano
> que cuando Muerte en él puso la mano,
> de la vida mayor fué Muerte muerta.

(R, 30)

At the start of the *canción, A Cristo crucificado,* the poet states clearly
and precisely his situation:

> Si al pie de vuestra cruz y a vos en ella,
> antes que se os arranque el alma santa,
> os presento, Señor, la canción mía...

(R, 33)

---

[11] *Francisco de Aldana, el Divino Capitán,* pp. 159-60.
[12] *A Literary History of Spain,* p. 88.

Indeed the poem is characterized by an insistent focussing on the details of the scene, a feature that parallels the tendency in the Ignatian scheme to recreate the event painstakingly with the mind's eye. In Aldana's poem, such an intensive focus is the basis for a curiously ironic, even cruelly humorous, understanding of the Crucifixion: [13]

> haced cuenta que el lodo
> os arrojo a la cara y estad quedo,
> que cuando yo lo doy, doy lo que puedo;          20
> vos habéis de esperalle,
> pues manos no tenéis para quitalle.
>
> (34)

> No me torzáis el rostro, estadme atento,          45
> que están esas espinas de mi parte
> porque no os retiréis hacia el madero...
>
> (35)

This form of direct, colloquial address is reminiscent of Lope's *Rimas sacras* and of the anonymous sonnet «No me mueve, mi Dios, el verte», but it cannot be confidently asserted that the Ignatian influence is more than a trace or an unconscious trait.

Other religious compositions provide parallels with rather than conscious imitation of Aldana's contemporaries. The opening of his *soneto* XXXVIII recalls the minor mystical poem of San Juan de la Cruz, «Que bien sé yo la fonte que mana y corre»:

> Sacrosanta, inmortal fuente que sales
> de Dios, de quien manaste eternamente,
> cuya llaneza es tal que, siendo fuente
> de Dios, el mismo Dios eres y vales...
>
> (R, 27)

But Aldana seldom approaches the kind of apprehension encountered in San Juan's major poems in his religious poetry, though the more philosophically-rooted *Carta para Arias Montano* is another matter, as we shall see. In some respects, though, his standpoint is near that of Fray Luis de León especially as the attitude is one of aspiration rather than attainment. The poem of Aldana that most resembles the work of the Augustinian is his sonnet, *Al cielo* (*soneto* XXXVII), a piece that Longfellow greatly admired: [14]

---

[13] For RIVERS, the *canción* is articulated in a «tono de fingida y blasfema crueldad» (*Francisco de Aldana, el Divino Capitán*, p. 165); RUIZ SILVA, while not going as far as this, believes the poem to comprise «una extraña mezcla de piedad y falta de respeto que otorga a los versos una dimensión de retorcimiento y un cierto carácter lúdico» (*Estudios sobre Francisco de Aldana*, p. 79).

[14] «In what glowing language he describes the aspirations of the soul for its paternal Heaven — its celestial home! — how beautifully portrays in a few lines the strong

Clara fuente de luz, nuevo y hermoso,
rico de luminarias, patrio Cielo,
casa de la verdad sin sombra o velo,
de inteligencias ledo, almo reposo:
   ¡oh cómo allá te estás, cuerpo glorioso,
tan lejos del mortal caduco velo,
casi un Argos divino alzado a vuelo,
de nuestro humano error libre y piadoso!
   ¡Oh patria amada!, a ti sospira y llora
esta en su cárcel alma peregrina,
llevada errando de uno en otro instante;
   esa cierta beldad que me enamora
suerte y sazón me otorgue tan benina
que, do sube el amor, llegue el amante.

(R, 26)

Both the impulse and the experience of this poem are akin to that of Luis de León's *Noche serena:* the poet contemplates the night sky and is moved by its beauty and grandeur to ponder on the contrast of Heaven and earth, the ideal and the illusory of Platonic thought. But in its realization, in particular its use of imagery, it is strikingly different. The opening of Fray Luis's poem establishes a contrast between the heavenly and the earthly clearly and symmetrically:

Cuando contemplo el cielo,
de innumerables luces adornado,
y miro hacia el suelo
de noche rodeado,
en sueño y en olvido sepultado... [15]

Even the rhyme-words of this first stanza can be paired within the dichotomy: «cielo-suelo», «adornado-sepultado». But the opening section of the poem is dominated by a contrast based on a single metaphor: that of buildings or dwellings. It is in the third stanza that it is most clearly enunciated and it can be seen that many of the antitheses of the poem (for example, darkness and light, glory and misery) relate to it. The soul, residing in a gloomy little cell looks upward at the abode of light and beauty:

—Morada de grandeza,
templo de claridad y hermosura,
el alma, que a tu alteza
nació, ¿qué desventura
la tiene en esta cárcel baja, escura?

desire, the ardent longing of the exiled and imprisoned spirit to wing its flight away and be at rest!». «Spanish Devotional and Moral Poetry», quoted in CRAWFORD, «Francisco de Aldana: A Neglected Poet», p. 48.

[15] I quote from *Poesías,* ed. ORESTE MACRÍ (Barcelona: Editorial Crítica, 1982), pp. 217-18.

A similar contrast also appears in Aldana's sonnet, though not as directly nor in such a structurally obvious manner: the «cárcel» of line 10 is semantically more the antithesis of «casa de la verdad» in line 3 rather than of the immediately preceding image of the «patria amada». But, more importantly, Aldana's utilization of imagery is radically different to Luis de León's. Rather than present a dominant motif, he employs, even within the narrow confines of a sonnet, several distinct metaphors. The heavens and, by extension, Heaven are, variously, a fountain, a house, a body, Argos, and a homeland. This constant changing of metaphor creates an impression of restlessness that is apt for the notion of a questing soul and which, furthermore, suggests that the perspective is predominantly that of the poet sighing and weeping nostalgically for his first, spiritual homeland. Luis de León's poem is, as its title implies, ultimately more tranquil. It concludes with a beatific vision of the Empyrean from which all traces of the earlier darkness and melancholy have been banished:

> ¡Oh campos verdaderos!
> ¡Oh prados con verdad frescos· y amenos!
> ¡Riquísimos mineros!
> ¡Oh deleitosos senos!
> ¡Repuestos valles de mil bienes llenos!

Aldana's metaphors are not only varied but also, in some cases, unexpected. The very opening of the sonnet with its reference to a fountain of light surprises. This is an uncommon and brilliant metaphor, whose connotations of movement and ascent perhaps anticipate the idea of flight later in the poem. It is enhanced by the epithet «nuevo» with its associations of freshness, of suddenly apprehended experience. The first metaphor of the second quatrain is treated in such a way as to create an unusual twist. Aldana not only refers to the night sky as a glorious body —another uncommon metaphor— but also avoids using the same word («cuerpo») in the following line where it could figure literally, and instead uses a periphrasis —«mortal caduco velo»— whose effect is increased by the fact that the term «cuerpo» has just been used as a metaphor. The imaginative inventiveness of the mythological allusion to Argos is consolidated by the powerful close of the quatrain with its two contrasting adjectives, deceptively joined by the coordinating conjunction —«libre y piadoso»— with its further association of a godhead, at once distant and compassionate. The first tercet contains a paradox: the notion of the soul trapped in its cell and yet able to stray. The experience of mortal life as both aimless and restless is thus powerfully conveyed. The final tercet is more hopeful, however, and this is reflected perhaps in the structural symmetry of the last two lines with balancing substantives in the penultimate line and parallel phrasing in the last line («suerte y sazón»; «sube el amor, llegue el amante»).

109

The other sonnet singled out by Longfellow (*soneto* XXXVI), also opens with a reference to the starry sky, though it thereafter differs from the poem just considered:

> Señor, que allá de la estrellada cumbre
> todo lo ves en un presente eterno,
> mira tu hechura en mí, que al ciego Infierno
> la lleva su terrena pesadumbre.
> Eterno Sol, ya la encendida lumbre
> do esté mi alegre abril florido y tierno
> muere, y ver pienso al más nevado invierno
> más verde la raíz de su costumbre.
> En mí tu imagen mira, ¡oh Rey Divino!,
> con ojos de piedad, que al dulce encuentro
> del rayo celestial verás volvella,
> que a verse como en vidrio cristalino
> la imagen mira el que se espeja dentro,
> y está en su vista dél su mirar della.
>
> (R, 26)

This is more explicitly a penitential poem, a plea for salvation, similar to the *salmos* of Quevedo's *Heráclito cristiano*. Indeed the second quatrain offers a lexical parallel to the following lines from the second poem of Quevedo's collection:

> Un año se me va tras otro año,
> y yo más duro y pertinaz porfío,
> por mostrarme más verde mi albedrío
> la torcida raíz do está mi daño. [16]

The tercets, however, breathe the more rarified air of Neoplatonic mysticism: as Ruiz Silva has pointed out, the «dulce encuentro» recalls both León Hebreo and San Juan de la Cruz's *Cántico espiritual*, [17] and, it could be added, the Echo myth in the *Carta para Arias Montano*. But for all its emotional breadth, the sonnet is perhaps less successful than *Al cielo* because it is less cohesive as a unit and because of some obscurity of meaning in the second quatrain. Ruiz Silva indeed goes so far as to suggest that due to what he assumes to be Cosme's editorial carelessness, «el soneto original de Aldana tenía que diferir del que ha llegado a nosotros» (p. 131). But even so, he does not comment on what seems to me the most problematic line in the poem: the eighth («más verde la raíz de su costumbre»). The preceding lines appear to express an awareness of the passing of time by means of an obvious symbolic reference to the seasons. The poet's youth, the springtime of his life, is fading and he already catches a glimpse of the

---

[16] *Ed. cit.*, p. 20.
[17] *Estudios sobre Francisco de Aldana*, p. 131.

winter of old age, without mentioning intervening summer and autumn. This accelerated or condensed vision of time is a feature that is to haunt Quevedo in his moral and metaphysical poetry, including, again, some of the poems in the *Heráclito cristiano*. The gist of these lines is thus reasonably clear but their details present difficulties. The first problem concerns the phrase «encendida lumbre». There is a pun here in that it follows the address to God as «Eterno Sol», but its precise significance is elusive. It may refer merely to the fire of youth, or more specifically, to the fire of love and the idea of love as a sinful pursuit, in which case, the «nevado invierno» may be understood not only, or not so much, as old age but as the punishment for a sinful youth. This latter interpretation has something to be said for it: the «nevado invierno» would follow on from the «ciego Infierno» —a near-homophone at a similar position in the first quatrain— and, furthermore, would clarify some of the semantic and morphological difficulties of the eighth line. The subject of the possessive pronoun «su» would be «lumbre»; the habit would be that of persevering in sinful love, even while aware of the outcome and its consequences; «verde» would then be doubly significant: both inexperience or an inability to learn from experience, and lasciviousness. By this interpretation, it is possible to discern a sense of progression. The general observations of the first quatrain are succeeded by a more specific and personal perspective in the second. It has to be admitted, though, that the effect of the second quatrain is to detract from the directness that the poet seemed to be aiming at from the opening. Somewhere in the compositional process it seems that Aldana has mistaken obscurity for complexity and not even the possibility of editorial neglect altogether rules this out.

Far less ambitious is the sonnet entitled *Hacimiento de gracias a Dios,* where the poet's awareness of his unworthiness leads to an expression of gratitude at God's creation and His mercy. But this falls a long way short of the inspirational *Carta para Arias Montano:*

> De otros tantos, gran Dios, cielos y estrellas,
> con cuanta allá luz y virtud se encierra,
> de otro sol, luna, fuego, aire, agua y tierra,
> con cuanto obráis acá vos, ellos y ellas,
>     deudor os soy, ¡oh deudas que entendellas
> no puede el ser mortal, pues frágil yerra!,
> y al mismo os debo a quien, en paz y en guerra,
> distes el cetro y la diadema dellas.
>     Deudor (mi sumo bien, ¿qué digo o hago?),
> deudor os soy del precio noble y alto
> de la Sangre filial, ¡oh inmenso abismo!
>     Pues ¿qué dará quien tanto os debe en pago?
> Doy lo que soy por vos, y en lo que falto,
> pague vuestro saber de sí a sí mismo.

(R, 31)

111

This sonnet shows up some of Aldana's characteristic failings: the unimaginative and mechanical use of enumeration, as in the first quatrain, and the tendency to labour an idea or a word, in this case the notion of indebtedness as seen in numerous derived words («deudor», «debo», «deudas», etc.). These traits bear witness perhaps to the fact that the sonnet, like a number of Aldana's religious poems (though maybe not as many as Ruiz Silva implies), does not tap deep or unexpected reserves of experience. Such a judgement may seem harsh if we remember the mediocre religious poetry of the likes of Góngora and Quevedo, but it is a judgement to a large degree emanating from the extraordinary expressive and emotional resonance of other poems by Aldana which, if not as overtly religious, nevertheless concern themselves with spiritual matters, indeed with nothing less than spiritual adventure. In such poems, to which I shall turn in the following chapter, the poet does not stand back or only relate to a scene or emotional context in an artificial manner. It is more like the situation in the *Otavas sobre el Juicio Final* where, for a moment, the poet ceases to be a mere observer, and describes how he too goes with the dead to be judged:

Mil gentes levantar ya veo los ojos 65
acá y allá con rostros de difuntos,
otros pedir a Dios de sus enojos
perdón, piedad, y gracia todos juntos;
ya viene cada cual con sus manojos
de espigas, sin perder granos ni puntos, 70
y yo también, ¡oh Dios terrible y santo!,
en las manos me iré con otro tanto.

(R, 137-38)

112

# 7

# THE INNER WORLD: FROM THE MORALIST TO
# THE MYSTIC

Just as in the *Otavas sobre el Juicio Final,* so too in the *Otavas dirigidas al rey don Felipe* there occurs a point in the poem where the poet unexpectedly intrudes. The latter composition, it will be remembered, is cast in the form of a double personification but when, in the course of a sweeping view of the international scene, the problem of the Low Countries is brought up, Aldana abruptly changes tack. He momentarily abandons the allegorical device and has recourse to autobiography: [1]

Mas dudo, ¡ay triste!, a Belgia, cuyo suelo
quiero y puedo afirmar no vanamente
haber de sangre yo rebelde al Cielo    555
teñido alguna vez, con ira ardiente;
otra despues quedó mi frágil velo
tendido en él con húmida corriente
del mismo humor, según o mala o buena
voluntad del destino al hombre ordena.    560

(R, 121)

---

[1] A similarly unexpected autobiographical intrusion occurs in the first section of the *Otavas en diversas materias* which relates the tale of Mars, Venus and Vulcan. For one stanza the poet interrupts the narrative to establish a direct analogy between Mars's sadness and his own amatory misfortunes:

Marte sabras, Ay de mi desgracia triste,
En ser yo relator de aquesta historia,
Que el dia que de tu Venus te partiste
Te fue como partir de su memoria:    60
Contra el Germano entre los Belgas fuiste
Por mas acumular gloria a tu gloria,
Y la madre de Amor do el Arno riega
Va de vn Satyro vil de Amores ciega.

(OC, II, 137)

The reference to Germans and Belgians, within this autobiographical framework, also effectively establishes 1567 as the *terminus a quo* for at least this part of the *Otavas en diversas materias,* a date that lends support to my speculations regarding the date of this poem in Chapter 1 (pp. 19-20).

Here Aldana alludes to a wound he suffered almost certainly at the siege of Alkmaar in 1573. [2] But of greater interest is the phrase applied to his description of the soldier's profession: «rebelde al Cielo.» This critical and negative view is of course radically distinct to the dominant theme of the poem, which urges prompt action against Spain's many enemies and which in several places exalts and sanctifies the shedding of blood:

> Despierte, pues, la gente bautizada
> del de Holofernes grave sueño insano 770
> antes que corte la enemiga espada
> el reclinado cuello del cristiano.
> No padezcamos cruz mal aplicada
> con el ladrón de la siniestra mano:
> vamos a la derecha, y destos fríos 775
> miembros corran a Dios sangrientos ríos.
>
> (129)

But though the disillusionment with warfare is only a passing, hardly noticeable, feature in the *Otavas dirigidas al rey don Felipe,* it is to be prominent in other poems. There is such a passage near the start of the *Carta para Arias Montano:*

> Oficio militar profeso y hago,
> ¡baja condenación de mi ventura!,
> que al alma dos infiernos da por pago: 15
> los huesos y la sangre que Natura
> me dió para vivir, no poca parte
> dellos y della he dado a la locura,
> mientras el pecho al desenvuelto Marte
> tan libre di que sin mi daño puede, 20
> hablando la verdad, ser muda el arte...
>
> (R, 57-58)

What these lines and the phrase «rebelde al Cielo» from the poem to Philip II express is not only disillusionment but condemnation: the soldier's life is not only unpleasant but wrong, hence the «dos infiernos» and the idea that such an activity is alien to God's wishes. An awareness of these passages is necessary for an understanding of one of Aldana's most celebrated and controversial poems, *soneto* XXX:

> Otro aquí no se ve que, frente a frente,
> animoso escuadrón moverse guerra,
> sangriento humor teñir la verde tierra,
> y tras honroso fin correr la gente;

---

[2] RIVERS (*Poesías,* p. 142n) refers to a variant reading in the title of the *Diálogo entre cabeza y pie* in the 1589 and 1593 editions which states that Aldana was wounded at the siege of Haarlem, rather than Alkmaar. Cosme subsequently corrected this to Alkmaar and indeed refers in other places to Francisco being wounded at Alkmaar.

éste es el dulce son que acá se siente:
«¡España, Santiago, cierra, cierra!»,
y por süave olor, que el aire atierra,
humo de azufre dar con llama ardiente;
   el gusto envuelto va tras corrompida
agua, y el tacto sólo apalpa y halla
duro trofeo de acero ensangrentado,
   hueso en astilla, en él carne molida,
despedazado arnés, rasgada malla:
¡oh solo de hombres digno y noble estado!

(R, 23)

Here the poet paints the horrors of war in detail; indeed Rivers has pointed to the likely influence of the Ignatian scheme of meditation.[3] Ruiz Silva has shown how the sonnet was misinterpreted by critics sympathetic to the imperialist vision of the Spain of the Austrias in the period immediately following the Civil War.[4] His own view is broadly in line with those of Rivers and Karl Vossler: that the poem is a denunciation of war. He shows convincingly how the enumerative technique —in this instance a telling and expressive device— prepares for the surprising and ironic final line:

> Y es el último verso precisamente —con su rotunda regulación yámbica— el que remata y da conciencia crítica a toda la composición. Después de habernos pintado toda una serie de horrores, que los cinco sentidos van registrando en una graduación descendente (vista, oído, olfato, gusto y tacto), nos dice: esto es, es esta espantosa crueldad, lo que el mundo glorifica (pp. 121-22).

But Ruiz Silva's reference to Aldana's modernity and the comparison of his approach to that of Wilfred Owen perhaps overlooks an important point. The impression this critic gives both here and in his chapter on Aldana's political poetry (pp. 179-95) is that of a personality torn by conflicting views: «me parece razonable decir que dos actitudes contradictorias —una más confesional, clarividente y moderna expresada además de modo muy hermoso, y otra oficial, intransigente y reaccionaria, expuesta sin belleza— coexisten en la obra del poeta» (p. 193).[5] I believe, however, that it is possible to understand Aldana's denunciation of war more in the context of his own day, and in the light of other poems by him. In particular, the important final line («¡oh solo de hombres digno y noble estado!») may be considered alongside the opening of a religious sonnet in which Aldana speaks of man's unwillingness to turn to his Creator:

---

[3] *Francisco de Aldana, el Divino Capitán*, pp. 159-60.
[4] *Estudios sobre Francisco de Aldana*, p. 121.
[5] A similar view was also expressed by CERNUDA: «Cierto que Aldana, en unos versos que dirige a Felipe II, manifiesta gran opinión acerca de la carrera del soldado; mas comparando dicha composición con un pasaje de la "Epístola a Arias Montano", la contradicción es evidente, y no semeja difícil decidir que este pasaje comunica su expresión más sincera y conclusiva, además de tener un valor poético que los otros versos no tienen.» «Tres poetas metafísicos», p. 113.

¡Oh indigno de la vida acá en el suelo,
oh del propio vivir ciego homicida,
quien al Supremo Autor de toda vida
no aspira con vital y ardiente celo!

(R, 31)

There is a lexical affinity between this and the last line of *soneto* XXX, and of significance too is Aldana's view of the man who does not aspire to God as «del propio vivir ciego homicida»; in other words, the metaphor is that of a soldier engaged in the destruction of life. If we apply this understanding to the last line of *soneto* XXX, then what Aldana seems to be condemning primarily is not war but man and man's pursuit of an activity that deflects him from his true mission, which is that of the quest for spiritual values. The line is phrased so as to throw the weight of the meaning upon the word «hombres», and the implication is that it is only by an inordinate attachment to mortal pursuits that one could conceive of such horror as «digno y noble». Such a reading does not emphasize as much as Ruiz Silva's the modern, anti-war aspect, but rather relates more to the *contemptus mundi* ideas of Aldana's day. In such a vein are Garcilaso's dismissive or, at least, negative allusions to war in passages from both his *Elegías,* in which he expresses a sense of world-weariness and defeat.[6] One also thinks of Luis de León's description of the emotional condition achieved by withdrawal from the bustle of worldly pursuits: «libre de amor,

[6] Cf.

¿A quién ya de nosotros el eceso
de guerras, de peligros y destierro
no toca y no ha cansado el gran proceso?
¿Quién no vio desparcir su sangre al hierro
del enemigo? ¿Quién no vio su vida
perder mil veces y escapar por yerro?...
¿Qué se saca d'aquesto? ¿Alguna gloria?
¿Algunos premios o agradecimiento?
Sabrálo quien leyere nuestra historia:
veráse allí que como polvo al viento,
así se deshará nuestra fatiga
ante quien s'endereza nuestro intento.

(*Ed. cit.,* pp. 101-02)

and:

¡Oh crudo, oh riguroso, oh fiero Marte,
de túnica cubierta de diamante
y endurecido siempre en toda parte!,
¿qué tiene que hacer el tierno amante
con tu dureza y áspero ejercicio,
llevado siempre del furor delante?
Ejercitando por mi mal tu oficio,
soy reducido a términos que muerte
será mi postrimero beneficio...

(*Ed. cit.,* p. 112)

de celo, / de odio, de esperanzas, de recelo». [7] Not only does he eschew the apparent pleasures of life but also the more immediately unpleasant aspects —jealousy, fear and hatred. The point is made emphatically too in Aldana's own *Otavas sobre el bien de la vida retirada*. The poet in his retreat stands aloof not only from the illusory pleasures of life but also from the travails of battle:

> No de Marte feroz, bravo, impaciente
> veré la confusión, la muerte y pena,        250
> ni veré que mi espada se ensangriente
> de propria sangre o de la sangre ajena;
> ni en medio del verano más ardiente,
> cuando Aquilón su helado soplo enfrena,
> sin aliento, sin vida y sin sentido,        255
> verme he de sangre y de sudor teñido.
>
> (R, 98)

War, then, like other human activities is folly; indeed in the *Carta para Arias Montano* it is «la locura» (R, 58). In short, what *soneto* XXX and the other criticisms of military life reveal is that the negative view can be explained by reference to a common enough concern in the moral poetry of the period.

But this does not mean that we should overlook the particular intensity of the expression nor that we should regard the resultant conflict of views as a conventional antithesis entailing involvement and renunciation. These passages hint at a deep-rooted awareness by the poet of his existence and its significance. Abundant evidence for this is to be found in a remarkable group of moral sonnets where the poet reveals more directly than elsewhere the presence of doubts and crisis, albeit in general rather than specific terms. The following poem is one of the bleakest Aldana ever wrote:

> Mil veces callo que romper deseo
> el cielo a gritos, y otras tantas tiento
> dar a mi lengua voz y movimiento,
> que en silencio mortal yacer la veo;
>    anda cual velocísimo correo
> por dentro al alma el suelto pensamiento
> con alto y de dolor lloroso acento,
> casi en sombra de muerte un nuevo Orfeo.
>    No halla la memoria o la esperanza
> rastro de imagen dulce y deleitable
> con que la voluntad viva segura:
>    cuanto en mí hallo es maldición que alcanza,
> muerte que tarda, llanto inconsolable,
> desdén del Cielo, error de la ventura.
>
> (R, 24)

[7] *Vida retirada*, 11. 39-40 (*ed. cit.*, p. 204).

The sense of dejection, abandonment and spiritual emptiness is conveyed memorably in the comparison of the soul to a «sombra de muerte» (1. 8) but the final tercet, weighty yet direct, is where there seems to be a remorseless focussing on these emotions. Here the poet employs enumeration in a masterly way by varying his phraseology so as to achieve a carefully structured effect. He cites five ideas or emotional states, grouped around the central «llanto inconsolable» (the shortest phrase in the list) and the writing, though apparently spontaneous, is rigorously balanced: the first two substantives are qualified by a clause, the fourth and fifth —the last two— by an adjectival phrase. Notable too is the contrast in intent between the first two phrases, achieved by the conflicting associations of the verbs: «alcanza» with its suggestion of movement, so that the whole phrase implies menace and even harassment, and «tarda» with its connotation of the static, of the purposelessness of life, seen as a living, somehow endless, death.

Indeed a judicious choice of verb is also seen at the start of the sonnet. Here the poet describes his inability to articulate the extent of his emotional despondency. The circumlocution in the first two lines is rich in significance. Most obviously it expresses the poet's desire for release for his pent-up feelings. But the verb «romper» also suggests a wish for destruction, as though the poet were lashing out in response to the emotional ills that beset him. Moreover, though the word «cielo» (1. 2) means sky or heavens rather than Heaven, the latter meaning may, in retrospect, cross the reader's mind after seeing the word «Cielo» in the last line. It might seem, with hindsight, then, that the poet is suggesting at the start, albeit in a veiled form, the idea of complaint at his fate, and more precisely, of an anger directed at Heaven, especially in view of the context in which «Cielo» is to figure below («desdén del Cielo»).

The variety of expression adopted by Aldana in this sonnet is another striking feature. Both the opening with its approximation to natural speech-patterns, as shown by the *enjambements* at the first and second lines, and the final tercet have an uncomplicated directness. But in the second quatrain, Aldana introduces a mythological allusion. This is a daring image of self-examination that is continued into the first tercet. Ruiz Silva takes a different view of this image: he interprets the object of the thought's search as a voice that is imprisoned in the hell of the poet's soul. But the first tercet, which continues with the analogy of Orpheus and Eurydice, surely implies that the aim of the poet's quest is something of greater import than the possibility or ability for self-expression, for he suggests that what he seeks will transform his existence. The problem resides in the vagueness of the term «imagen dulce y deleitable». On the figurative level it clearly refers to Eurydice but what this represents for the *persona* is not altogether certain. Indeed the epithets are such that an amatory association cannot be ruled out, although it is more likely that it points to a state of emotional stability and well-being which the poet has not only lost but which he can neither recollect having experienced nor conceivably hope to attain: not a trace of it is to be found either in his memory or in his expectation. As an expression of disenchantment and hopelessness, this poem is without equal.

The other three sonnets of this group are all in differing ways sequels to the one just considered. They not only allude to the same spiritual or emotional malaise but also suggest a remedy or a resolution. The following sonnet begins with the same negative view of experience:

> ¡Ay, que considerar el bajo punto
> del estado mortal al alma hiere!,
> mas del tal peso alienta y la requiere
> alta contemplación de su trasunto;
> pero con esto el gran rector conjunto
> aquel tributo contrapuesto infiere
> do no con celo tanto el bien se quiere
> cuanto a la humana parte el mal va junto.
> No sé si, al sostener la fatigosa
> vida, fuera mejor falto jüicio,
> con que el dolor se engaña y no se siente,
> o si sentir en todo toda cosa,
> con tal daño del alma y perjüicio,
> es más alivio a la pasión doliente.
>
> (R, 24)

The poem is informed by a Neoplatonic vision of life and a key dichotomy of that philosophy: the «bajo punto» of mortal existence is opposed by the idea of a higher reality. Consequently, there is here, unlike in the previous sonnet, a sense of purpose and the possibility of transcendence. But this is a knowledge that is not without its drawbacks. There is, in fact, an important and unexpected twist in the argument of the poem. In the first quatrain the awareness of the ideal («trasunto») is viewed as the alleviation of the wretched condition in which the poet finds himself. Towards the end of the second quatrain, however, the poet implies the experiencing of an opposite truth: that such an awareness involves a realization of the limitations of human life. He thus finds himself in a dilemma: the solace initially expected from the contemplation of a higher reality vanishes when it is realized that this entails a full awareness of the very condition from which the poet has longed to escape. Both the development of the argument in this sonnet and the anguish caused by the clash of philosophy and experience anticipate some of the moral and amatory sonnets of Quevedo. [8]

The tercets elaborate upon the dilemma and express the poet's perplexity: is ignorance of one's condition to be preferred to painful apprehension?

[8] Notably the sonnet «Todo tras sí lo lleva el año breve» (ed. cit., p. 32) with its reluctant adherence to a Stoic tenet («mas si es ley, y no pena, ¿que me aflijo?»); and the amatory sonnet «Mandóme, ¡ay Fabio!, que la amase Flora» (ibid., 361) where there is a less than wholehearted acceptance of a Platonic view of love, seemingly imposed upon the poet.

The doubts and questions in these lines are expressed in some marvellously eloquent phrases. The first tercet begins with four monosyllables which, allied to the alliteration on *s*, produce an effect of stammering, of verbal as well as rational confusion. The phrase «sostener la fatigosa / vida» evokes powerfully the idea of life as a burden, reinforced as it is by the strong *enjambement* and the following alliteration on *f* and *j*. No less effective is the first line of the final tercet with its climactic near-repetition («todo toda») —evidence of a poet skilled and mature enough to make even the arrangement of simple words an instrument of poetic depth.

No doubts are manifested in *soneto* XXXI. The keynote is aspiration as in the sonnet *Al Cielo* considered in the previous chapter, though in the present poem the accent is more personal and the remedy is envisaged in more specific terms:

> El ímpetu crüel de mi destino
> ¡como me arroja miserablemente
> de tierra en tierra, de una en otra gente,
> çerrando a mi quietud siempre el camino!
> ¡Oh si tras tanto mal grave y contino,
> roto su velo mísero y doliente,
> el alma con un vuelo diligente
> volviese a la región de donde vino,
> iríame por el cielo en compañía
> del alma de algún caro y dulce amigo
> con quien hice común acá mi suerte:
> ¡oh qué montón de cosas le diría,
> cuáles y cuántas, sin temer castigo
> de fortuna, de amor, de tiempo y muerte!

(R, 23)

But the standpoint is nonetheless that of one who is still some way short of the Promised Land: the refuge from the poet's present ills is conceived only as a hypothesis as shown by the conditional clause and tenses. Indeed the first quatrain is a cry from the heart, once more realized in lines of outstanding craftsmanship. The idea of the poet being driven along or buffeted by fate is present in the verb «arroja» and reflected in the rhythm of the sonnet's opening with its precipitous proparoxytone («ímpetu»). [9] By contrast, the second line ends with the ponderous six-syllable word «miserablemente» that prepares for the sense of aimlessness that is to be conveyed in

---

[9] GARCILASO, *Canción* IV, ll. 7-12:

> pues soy por los cabellos arrastrado
> de un tan desatinado pensamiento
> que por agudas peñas peligrosas,
> por matas espinosas,
> corre con ligereza más que el viento,
> bañando de mi sangre la carrera.

(*Ed. cit.*, p. 87)

the following line whose binary form involves the repetition of the formula «de ... en» hinting at the sameness of life. The use of the image of the path in line 4 has ironic implications: the opening has described the poet borne along by the force of fate, but movement and progression are unfortunately suspended when the poet sees or thinks of the way that leads to peace of mind («quietud»).

The second quatrain expresses a commonplace of Neoplatonic philosophy: the soul's capacity to return to its source («la región de donde vino») as in Luis de León's *Oda a Francisco Salinas:*

> A cuyo son divino
> el alma, que en olvido está sumida,
> torna a cobrar el tino
> y memoria perdida
> de su origen primera esclarecida.[10]

Common to both poems also is the notion of the flight or ascent of the soul, freed from its mortal attachment of the body, though the periphrasis employed by Aldana for the body is characteristically his. There is a further point of contact between these poems: the idea of friendship. Towards the end of the Leonine Ode the poet appeals to his friends to join him in the contemplation of the divine:

> A este bien os llamo,
> gloria del apolíneo sacro coro,
> amigos, a quien amo
> sobre todo tesoro,
> que todo lo visible es triste lloro.

The identity of the friend referred to in Aldana's sonnet is not clear, though it could be Arias Montano as in the verse epistle. Apart from the spiritual aspiration —represented by the notion of transcendence— there is in the final tercet a hint of another remedy or course of action: that of withdrawal. The benefits of seclusion are essentially liberation from the extremes and fluctuations of emotion, very much as in the lines from Luis de León's *Vida retirada* quoted earlier (ll. 39-40). This theme is to preoccupy Aldana in the *Carta para Arias Montano* but it is present too in the final sonnet of the group I have been considering:

> En fin, en fin, tras tanto andar muriendo,
> tras tanto variar vida y destino,
> tras tanto de uno en otro desatino
> pensar todo apretar, nada cogiendo,

[10] *Ed. cit.,* p. 207.

> tras tanto acá y allá yendo y viniendo
> cual sin aliento inútil peregrino,
> ¡oh Dios!, tras tanto error del buen camino,
> yo mismo de mi mal ministro siendo,
>
> hallo, en fin, que ser muerto en la memoria
> del mundo es lo mejor que en él se asconde,
> pues es la paga dél muerte y olvido,
>
> y en un rincón vivir con la vitoria
> de sí, puesto el querer tan sólo adonde
> es premio el mismo Dios de lo servido.

(R, 25)

There is a link between this sonnet and the previous one. It is recognizably a sequel, for in *soneto* XXXI the poet had indicated that his wretched condition («tanto mal grave y ·contino») was a present state from which escape was but a remote possibility. The opening of *soneto* XXXIV, however, makes it clear that his hope has been fulfilled. Moreover, there is a lexical similarity between the fifth line of *soneto* XXXI and the phraseology employed for the series of subordinate clauses in the present sonnet.[11] Again, as Ruiz Silva points out,[12] the poet utilizes verbs of movement to refer to the kind of pointless existence that he has now rejected. The tone is direct and the message a straightforward one, yet Aldana again manages some particularly expressive lines, notably the fifth with its internal assonance and rhyme («acá y allá», «yendo y viniendo») which produce an appropriate correlative for the notion of aimlessness, while the alliteration of *n* and *t* in the following line perhaps reflects the idea of breathlessness and lack of resolution, both meanings of «aliento» (breath and courage) being possible here.

In the tercets, the poet refers to the need for detachment from the worldly. This is perhaps the most ascetic of Aldana's realizations of this condition. There is no mention of the more positive aspects that could accrue from such a retreat: the benefits of friendship and the possibility of being able to contemplate the natural world. These ideas find their principal expression in what is probably Aldana's last poem, the *Carta para Arias Montano*, though he had touched on several issues connected with the scorn of the worldly in a poem written more than a decade earlier than the *Carta*: the *Otavas sobre el bien de la vida retirada*.

This poem has come down to us in an incomplete form, as indicated by the epigraph «faltan innumerables» at the end. There can be no doubt on this occasion about the accuracy of such an observation for the work indeed comes to an abrupt halt; moreover, the last five stanzas seem to be

---

[11] ALDANA may have been inspired by PETRARCH's *sonetto* XLVIII whose first two lines read: «Padre del ciel, dopo i perduti giorni,/dopo le notti vaneggiando spese». See D. G. WALTERS, «Three Examples of Petrarchism in Quevedo's *Heráclito cristiano*», *Bulletin of Hispanic Studies*, 58 (1981), 21-30 (at pp. 25-26).
[12] *Estudios sobre Francisco de Aldana*, p. 128.

pointing to a change of direction. The emphasis at the end is on the details of the pastoral ideal and less on the scorn of the worldly —both for its material and emotional drawbacks— of which the poet has previously given broad coverage. It is noticeable too that there is a distinct falling-away of inspiration in the final stanzas: the taut, precise manner of the earlier part is replaced by a more relaxed style. This does not of itself make for indifferent verse but lines like these from the last two stanzas are very lacklustre:

> entonces tú, pastor, con viva gana,                    325
> de tu zurrón manchado y vedejudo
> el pan, la fruta sacarás, y el queso;
> ¡dichosa fruta y pan, dichoso queso!
>
> ¿Qué fruta y pan ternás que no aproveche
> con tanto bien al alma descansada?                    330
> ¿O qué verás que el gusto al fin deseche
> de tan süave fruta y sazonada?
>
> (R, 100-01)

The ending as it stands then suggests a running out of steam or a loss of interest; it certainly does not seem that the recourse to pastoral at this late stage was a sound idea.

The theme of the poem is one of the most popular and conventional in sixteenth-century Spanish literature. It can be summed up by the title of one of the most seminal works of the century, Guevara's *Menosprecio de corte y alabanza de aldea*. One of the features of Aldana's poem is its comprehensiveness. He provides a broad survey of the ills of society: the desire for wealth, flattery, warfare, injustice, political conspiracy, the hollowness of court life, the melancholy illusion that is love —all these pass beneath the poet's critical gaze. In the *Otavas,* Aldana dedicates far less space than in the *Carta para Arias Montano* to the positive aspects that come with his idyllic retreat. Indeed the tentative closing stanzas in the pastoral vein perhaps represent a belated gesture in this direction. Another difference of emphasis between the two poems resides in the fact that the notion of friendship is but a passing idea in the earlier work. What distinguishes the two poems more than anything, however, is the standpoint of the poet. The *Otavas* enunciate a conventional, moral view of experience; the *Carta,* a more personal metaphysical vision.

It makes sound sense, then, not to view the earlier poem merely as a direct antecedent —a kind of trial run— for the *Carta.*[13] It also does more justice to the merits of the former if this connection is not made. For the

---

[13] This is the view of RUIZ SILVA (*ibid.,* p. 219), who suggests that the *Otavas* «puede ser considerado como un antecedente o incluso como un ensayo para su gran "Epístola a Montano"».

poem is not as diffuse as its unfinished state and breadth of coverage might imply. It has a purpose even a rigour about it. The opening stanza sets the tone; it is crisp and poised:

> Gózate, rey, subido allá en tu alteza
> de título real de nuevo Augusto;
> dilata y sube el son de tu grandeza
> del scita helado al etíope adusto;
> abunde el oro, abunde la riqueza,          5
> con jüicio o sin él, justo o no justo,
> y a mayor posesión, mayor codicia:
> haz de tu incierta ley cierta injusticia.

(R, 88)

The sense of symmetry, seen especially in the balancing *bimembre* lines, enables the dismissive message of this opening to be clearly, even classically, articulated. But the poem's cohesion is to be found mainly in a shrewd use of diction and imagery. At an obvious level it may be noted that the early part of the poem has a refrain that occurs at fairly regular intervals, drawing attention to the poet's withdrawal from the world: «Aquí me estoy» —a phrase that is always to be found in the first line of the stanzas in which it figures.

Of greater significance, however, is the way in which Aldana uses terminology for a dual, contrasting purpose. The opening line refers to a king (an imaginary or symbolic king here, not Philip II) in all his glory; the images employed express the notion of height: «subido», «alteza». In the fifth stanza, too, both terms are used. The king's palace is described as «ese edificio alto y pomposo / que va subiendo a la región del fuego» (89), a phrase that is echoed much later in the poem: «las plazas rodeadas / de soberbio, pomposo, alto edificio» (96). In the sixth stanza, Aldana refers to the instability of the king's power; again the notion of height is employed as he describes how the wheel of fortune operates: «para bajarte a mas ínfimo estado / de cuanto eres en alto colocado» (90). But words like «alto» and «subir» and their derivatives are also employed in an opposite connection or context to allude to the secluded life enjoyed by the poet and his companions. In the fourth stanza, there is a reference to the serenity of such an existence in the following terms:

> un ángel nuestras almas concertando
> va con jüicio alto y soberano          30
> y mezcla en tal quietud tan alto modo
> que en nosotros la parte es parte y todo.

(89)

Interesting here too is the use of the term «soberano», a word that primarily suggests the idea of kingship. In the eighth stanza there is a passage

124

which probably derives from the Biblical parable of the houses built on the sand and on the rock. The foundations of the poet's life, he claims, are established upon the latter: «Fundo mi habitación en valle amena / sobre *alta* piedra en un cimiento firme» (90) (my italics). In the same stanza he speaks of his aspiration to the eternal life by using the verb «subirme». Later in the poem there is a reference to God as «Señor del alto coro» (93). Indeed the contrast of kingship and divine government is pinpointed on a number of occasions by the utilization of images or phrases that imply a distinction between the true and the false or transient exercise of power and authority. Apart from the description of God as «Señor del alto coro» quoted above, we find the phrase «Señor de las supernas hierarquías» (92), while the poet, in his retreat, can contemplate the authority of God and how the natural world obeys:

> la mar profunda aquí enfrenada veo,                          85
> obediente al Señor del firmamento,
> do un aire fresco y dulce a maravilla
> las ondas va encrespando por la orilla.
>
> (91)

The device of using the one term or idea for a double, conflicting purpose can be seen too in the poet's treatment of the adjective «cortés». Its primary meaning relates to the negative side of the dichotomy embodjed in the poem, as in this sardonic description:

> No temeré jamás que el bel mancebo
> diligente, cortés, pomposo y largo,
> un Marte en armas y en la corte un Febo,          275
> de quien yo adoro me suceda al cargo...
>
> (98-99)

There had also been previously a mention of the «soberbio, altivo cortesa· no» (96). But very different is the association in these lines:

> Yo en este paraíso de mi vida
> gozo siempre aquel bien que el *cortés* Cielo
> da sólo al que con fe larga y crecida,          195
> con alto amor, con puro, ardiente celo,
> tiene a su eterno Autor el alma unida...
>
> (95-96) (my italics)

Here the term «cortés» is used unusually to refer to the munificence of a provident God. It may be noted too that the favoured concept of height appears in this passage, in the phrase «alto amor».

As a final example of the poet's keen awareness of semantic complexity in this work, there is a pun on the words «celeste» and «celestial» in successive stanzas early in the poem where the aim is once more to indicate an

125

opposite: in his idyllic retirement the poet enjoys «un celeste y dulce privilegio» (90) and he dwells in a place where he will not be struck by «el rayo celestial» (90). His constant recourse to such devices, especially in the early part of the work, lends it an air of purpose and coherence.

Unlike the *Otavas dirigidas al rey don Felipe,* the present poem has the knack of converting indignation into lines of powerful poetry. In these lines Aldana expresses his scorn of the tyrant:

> Viva el tirano allá, si nombrar vida     65
> se puede un duro y tímido recelo,
> y púrpura del Mar Tiro venida
> los miembros vista de su frágil velo;
> huya con alma inquieta y desabrida
> la grave punición del justo Cielo;     70
> dése a entender que entiende cuanto ignora,
> pues no es llegada aún la fatal hora.
>
> (91)

The first two lines are effectively deflating: the definition of «vida» serves to undermine the standard popular acclamation of rulers («viva»); while the use of hyperbaton in the fourth line reinforces the dismissive allusion to the body. In other places Aldana is direct and emphatic. He speaks of the fickleness of human love thus:

> Sin sentido y sin alma estar pareces,
> puesto en un cierto y claro devaneo,
> y de tu misma vida en ti careces,
> que allá se fué a vivir do está el deseo;     140
> contino en tu mudanza permaneces,
> sólo en mudable ser firme te veo;
> está tu vida, seso, alma y reposo
> transformado en un vil cuerpo asqueroso.
>
> (93)

In the last two lines Aldana makes maximum use of the rhythmic potential of the hendecasyllable: the staccato effect of the first of these lines is succeeded by the emphatic polysyllabic words («transformado», «asqueroso») in the next. By contrast with this direct approach, the preceding stanza had described the lover's unenviable condition by recourse to mixed metaphors:

> Breve y triste placer, largo tormento,
> vidrïosa esperanza, incierta vida,     130
> encogido temor, tibio contento,
> dura prisión y libertad perdida
> tienes, amante, allá por fundamento,
> con ser tú de ti mismo a ti homicida,
> haciendo siempre en esta mar sin calma     135
> de tu proprio dolor manjar al alma.
>
> (93)

Notable too is a stanza that describes the perils of those who venture to sea in search of wealth in far-off lands. This is, of course, a stock topic, but Aldana's realization is vivid particularly in a line where the restlessness of the gold-seekers is reflected in the stumbling and unpredictable metrical effect of a series of imperatives followed by the most violent of *enjambements* —across the one word. I quote the whole of the stanza concerned because of the parallels it offers with a passage on a similar subject in Luis de León's *Vida retirada:* [14]

> Tú que, entre el cielo raso y la mar yerma,
> puesto de amarga muerte en las honduras,
> corres huyendo la pobreza enferma,
> del polo examinando las alturas:
> corre, no pares, ve, camina, perma-  165
> neciendo siempre en tantas desventuras
> que mal podrá alcanzar tu pensamiento
> al inútil madero el mayor viento.
>
> (94-95)

Though it does not possess the sustained emotional depth and sophisticated structure of the Leonine Ode, [15] it can be safely said that the neglect suffered by the *Otavas sobre el bien de la vida retirada* is no reflection on its several, undoubted merits.

I turn lastly to what is by common consent Aldana's masterpiece — the *Carta del mismo Capitán Francisco de Aldana para Arias Montano sobre la contemplación de Dios y los requisitos della*. This poem seems to pick up where the group of moral sonnets considered earlier in the chapter had left off. After the initial, punning dedication or eulogy, the poet speaks of himself in terms that recall the opening of *soneto* XXXI and the conclusion of *soneto* XXXII with their allusions to the poet beset by misfortune. The simile of the withered leaf driven by the cruel wind is, in particular, reminiscent of the image of the poet suffering the buffetings of fate in the first two lines of *soneto* XXXI («El ímpetu crüel de mi destino / ¡cómo me arroja miserablemente»):

[14] Cf. *Vida retirada*, 11. 76-80:

> Y mientras miserable-
> mente se están los otros abrasando
> con sed insaciable
> del peligroso mando,
> tendido yo a la sombra esté cantando...
>
> (*Ed. cit.*, p. 205)

[15] I examine the interplay of theme and structure in *Vida retirada* in my article, «On the Structure, Imagery and Significance of *Vida retirada*», *Modern Language Review*, 81 (1986), 71-81.

yo soy un hombre desvalido y solo,
espuesto al duro hado cual marchita
hoja al rigor del descortés Eolo;
    mi vida temporal anda precita          10
dentro el infierno del común trafago
que siempre añade un mal y un bien nos quita.

(R, 57)

Later in the introductory section there is an echo of the keynote of
*soneto* XXXIV —a sense of moral discovery and disillusionment:

Mas ya, ¡merced del Cielo!, me desato,
ya rompo a la esperanza lisonjera
el lazo en que me asió con doble trato...      45

(59)

A notable feature of the first part of the *Carta* is its adherence, or at
least similarity, to some of the conventional formal elements of Renaissance
epic and pastoral poems. There is a direct address, involving a punning
allusion, a lengthy autobiographical passage —where the modesty topos is
subsumed by the poet's depiction of the miseries and trials he has endur-
ed— [16] and finally an expression of the work's intention, clearly enunciated
in two tercets:

pienso torcer de la común carrera
que sigue el vulgo y caminar derecho
jornada de mi patria verdadera;
    entrarme en el secreto de mi pecho
y platicar en él mi interior hombre,      50
do va, do está, si vive, o qué se ha hecho.

(59)

One is reminded of the method at the opening of, say, Garcilaso's *Eclogue* III, with its components of flattering dedication, autobiography, and
statement of intention («De cuatro ninfas que del Tajo amado / Salieron
juntas, a cantar me ofrezco»).

The opening section of the *Carta para Arias Montano* differs from the
corresponding parts in other verse epistles by Aldana. In these, he reveals
a certain uneasy self-consciousness about the need for a kind of organized
informality. The start of his *Respuesta a Cosme* is a case in point:

En amigable estaba y dulce trato,
trato amigable y dulce (si amigable
y dulce trato ser llamado puede
cosa que, ausente vos, venga a ofrecerse)...

(R, 48)

---

[16] ARTHUR TERRY suggests that in the phrase «callaré las causas de interese» (1. 28),
Aldana «is probably thinking of his personal difficulties in the Netherlands under the
governorship of Requesens, who replaced the Duque de Alba in 1573». *An Anthology
of Spanish Poetry*, p. 160.

The constant repetitions of «amigable», «dulce» and «trato» make for an affected, even irritating, opening. The first lines of the *Carta a Don Bernardino de Mendoza* are also unconvincing as they strive after informality via a search for the appropriate form of address:

> Ilustre hijo. No que son donzellas.
> Padre dire? Tampoco que son hijas,
> Del alto Ioue. Pues querido hermano?
> No que son nueve. Pues dichoso amante?
> No que son castas. Que podre deziros?            5
> Digo os amante, hermano, padre, hijo...
>
> (OC, I, 113)

But the more formal, even conventional, appearance of the start of the *Carta para Arias Montano* does not preclude a mode of more intimate, even spontaneous, address, in keeping with the freedom and flexibility that one may justly expect from the epistolary genre. This has been noted by two commentators on the poem. Arthur Terry is of the opinion that «the interplay between metrical structure and natural speech patterns is the driving force behind even the most intensely metaphysical passages of the poem». [17] A similar observation is made by Cernuda: «Aldana parece buscar en el verso... un equilibrio entre el ritmo métrico y el ritmo de la frase, bien visible en su uso del *enjambement,* de manera que no sea el primero, sino el segundo quien dirija el movimiento melódico». [18] The poem is furthermore able to accommodate a variety of expressive registers without any sense of stylistic discontinuity or incongruity. This is seen to good effect in the lines following the climax. The high point of the poem is a passage in which the poet endeavours to express the indefinible experience of God's love and the resultant union. It is the most clearly rhetorical passage in the whole work: an urgent interrogation followed by a carefully structured enumeration that proclaims the bounties afforded the soul and which culminates in an ecstatic exclamation. What preserves the momentum of the poem following this point is the sudden adoption of a colloquial manner:

> No más allá. Ni puedo, aunque lo quiera.        280
> Do la vista alcanzó, llegó la mano;
> ya se les cierra a entrambos la carrera.
> ¿Notaste bien, dotísimo Montano,
> notaste cuál salí, más atrevido
> que del cretense padre el hijo insano?          285
>
> (67)

There is no feeling of anti-climax but rather of a movement from a mode of self-communion to an attitude of confiding in a close and dear friend,

---

[17] *Ibid.,* p. 112.
[18] «Tres poetas metafísicos», p. 115.

who suddenly becomes the immediate audience and, presumably, the admiring and consoling companion. Such a movement is made to seem natural in the context of a poem in which friendship is a major theme, if not a motivating force. Indeed the lines quoted above serve as a seamless transition to a lengthy section in which the poet reiterates his praise of Montano.

Another way in which Aldana reconciles the informality of intimate communication with the formal requirements of a grand design can be seen in the manner in which he incorporates into even the most philosophical passages an equivalence for or an image of spontaneous intellectual excitement —of one warming to his argument. Phrases such as «Torno a decir» or «Digo que» are used to introduce ideas that are both conceptually and stylistically elaborate, for instance:

> Torno a decir que el pecho enamorado
> la celestial, de allá, rica inflüencia
> espere humilde, atento y reposado,
>    sin dar ni recebir propia sentencia
> que en tal lugar la lengua más despierta                    185
> es de natura error y balbucencia.
>
> (63)

and:

> Digo que, puesta el alma en su sosiego,
> espere a Dios cual ojo que cayendo
> se va sabrosamente al sueño ciego,
>    que al que trabaja por quedar durmiendo,            235
> esa misma inquietud destrama el hilo
> del sueño, que se da no le pidiendo...
>
> (65)

The opening of the poem illustrates Cernuda's point about «el ritmo de la frase» and the use of *enjambement:*

> Montano, cuyo nombre es la primera
> estrellada señal por do camina
> el Sol el cerco oblicuo de la esfera,
>    nombrado así por voluntad divina
> para mostrar que en ti comienza Apolo                    5
> la luz de su celeste disciplina...
>
> (57)

It is also highly significant as regards the thematic development of the poem. Two important images or image-groups arise from this opening and both involve punning. The first word of the poem («Montano») provides one of these images, that of the mountain. Aldana does not explain the pun at this point, being content to leave the one word resound as a brief, initial apostrophe. Indeed it is only in the latter part of the work, after the climactic section, that he enlarges upon the pun. In the first place, he alludes to mountains with mythological and Biblical associations:

> Tratar en esto es sólo a ti debido,
> en quien el Cielo sus noticias llueve
> para dejar el mundo enriquecido;
>     por quien de Pindo las hermanas nueve
> dejan sus montes, dejan sus amadas                    290
> aguas, donde la sed se mata y bebe,
>     y en el santo Sïón ya trasladadas,
> al profético coro por tu boca
> oyendo están, atentas y humilladas.
>
>                     (68)

As Arthur Terry has pointed out, these references are to Montano's Latin poems wherein Christian doctrine is contained within classical forms; [19] indeed, even in Montano's Spanish compositions, we find a similar blend, as in the opening of his poem to the Virgin, from which I quoted in the previous chapter, where the poet refers —by way of «non-invocation»— to mythological figures: «No invoco aquel napeo / coro que en el Parnaso hace su asiento, / ni al gran músico Orfeo.» [20] Later in this section praising Montano, Aldana refers to another mountain —«Un monte dicen que hay sublime y alto» (68). This is a symbolic rather than a real mountain: a place of freedom and purity, removed from the perils and miseries of the world («del mundo ajeno»). It is a kind of *locus amoenus:*

> todo es tranquilidad de fértil mayo,
> purísima del sol templada lumbre,
> de hielo o de calor sin triste ensayo.                318
>
>                     (69)

Next, Aldana makes clear the pun contained in the very first word of the poem («Montano»):

> Pareces tú, Montano, a la gran cumbre
> deste gran monte, pues vivir contigo               320
> es muerte de la misma pesadumbre...
>
>                     (69)

His friend Montano is seen not only as an ally and companion in his renunciation of the worldly and his quest for the contemplative ideal but also as an inspiration, even an indispensable agent, for attaining such a goal. At one point, indeed, the poet establishes an analogy between his relationship with

---

[19] *An Anthology of Spanish Poetry,* p. 161.
[20] *Fray Luis de León y la escuela salmantina,* p. 144.

Montano and the soul's longing to be united with the Creator, an idea that has been dominant in the principal section of the poem:

> El alma que contigo se juntare
> cierto reprimirá cualquier deseo     335
> que contra el proprio bien la vida encare...
>
> (69)

There follows a reference to Monte Urgull, the hill site of the fortress of San Sebastián where Aldana was governor at the time of the poem's composition. This —the third mountain image— is the location for the last part of the poem which is to consist of a remarkable description of the seashore near the fortress. But there is within this one scene —taken from a real, geographic location, not a symbolic one— a significant change of perspective. The last part of the poem suggests a descent from the lofty spiritual heights attained previously and sustained as an image by the persistent allusions to mountains. The notion of descent is explicitly stated:

> No busco monte excelso y soberano     355
> de ventiscosa cumbre en quien se halle
> la triplicada nieve en el verano;
> menos profundo, escuro, húmido valle
> donde las aguas bajan despeñadas
> por entre desigual, torcida calle...     360
>
> (70)

and later:

> Bajaremos allá de cuando en cuando,
> altas y ponderadas maravillas
> en recíproco amor juntos tratando...     375
>
> (71)

The poet invites his friend to leave the mountain-peak and join him in a study of the forms of marine life so fully and lovingly described in the closing section.

The whole process involving the poem's climax, the mountain imagery and the final descent to admire the beauty of God's creation suggests the stages of a mystical process. The soul withdraws from the world, ascends towards God, is absorbed by Him while still retaining its identity and, finally, through this union can now fully comprehend the beauties of the visible world. What seems to be detailed in Aldana's *Carta para Arias Montano*, then, is a fundamental tenet of San Juan de la Cruz's mystical verse: «conocer por Dios las criaturas, y no por las criaturas a Dios.» [21] The radiant

---

[21] *Vida y obras de San Juan de la Cruz*, biography by P. CRISÓGONO DE JESÚS, revised by P. Matías del Niño Jesús, edition of works by P. Lucinio del SS. Sacramento, 4th edn (Madrid: Biblioteca de Autores Cristianos, 1960), p. 1087.

sensuality at the close of *Noche oscura* and, to a lesser extent, *Cántico espiritual* —the way in which the senses appear to have been sanctified— has a parallel in the freshness and humility of Aldana's seashore description. In this, the mountain imagery has been a key element.

The remainder of the first six lines of the poem (i. e., all save the initial address «Montano») takes the form of what Arthur Terry has felicitously described as a «submerged pun». [22] Arias recalls Aries, the zodiacal sign that marks the beginning of Spring with the sun's entry into it. The sun, in fact, is to figure prominently in much of the metaphorical writing in the poem, and in a variety of ways. It is used as an illustration of God's powerful love:

> Puede del sol pequeña fuerza ardiente
> desde la tierra alzar graves vapores
> a la región del aire allá eminente,          120
>    ¿y tantos celestiales protectores,
> para subir a Dios alma sencilla,
> vernán a ejercitar fuerzas menores?

(61)

It also serves to demonstrate the soul's need to be passive, to wait patiently for God:

> No tiene que buscar los resplandores          220
> del sol quien de su luz anda cercado,
> ni el rico abril pedir hierbas y flores...

(65)

In the following quotation, Aldana recalls Ficino on the differing characteristics of the sun and the light it emits. [23] His purpose is to illustrate how the soul, though re-admitted to the One, does not thereby relinquish its being («no que ... / cese en el Hacedor de ser hechura»). On the contrary:

> mas como el aire, en quien en luz se estiende
> el claro sol, que juntos aire y lumbre
> ser una misma cosa el ojo entiende.          108

(61)

---

[22] *An Anthology of Spanish Poetry*, p. 159.
[23] This occurs in Chapter 13 of the Sixth Speech where Ficino discusses the light of truth in the soul and expands upon a passage in the Sixth Book of the *Republic* where PLATO compares the sun and God to each other to make the point that the latter is to our minds as the former is to our eyes: «The sun generates eyes and it bestows upon them the power to see. This power would be in vain, and would be overwhelmed by eternal darkness if the light of the sun were not present, imprinted with the colors and shapes of bodies. In this light the eye sees the colors and shapes of bodies, nor does the eye see anything else but light; it seems to see various things, however, because the light pouring into it is decorated with various forms of external bodies.» *Ed. cit.*, p. 206.

Aldana also relates the sun image to the emblem of the infinite sphere, already hinted at in the third line of the poem: «el cerco oblicuo de la esfera.» As Louise Salstad has shown, this emblem is employed to describe the contemplative experience and is supported by such metaphors for the union of the soul and God as the sea that envelops the fish and the heat contained within the fire. [24] The concepts of the centre and the revolutions around the centre find a profound realization in these lines that start with the simile of the fish:

> cual pece dentro el vaso alto, estupendo,     85
> del Océano irá su pensamiento
> desde Dios para Dios yendo y viniendo:
>     seróle allí quietud el movimiento,
> cual círculo mental sobre el divino
> centro, glorioso origen del contento...     90
>
> (60)

Passages such as these highlight Aldana's achievement as a philosophical poet: concise and passionate for all their intellectual rigour.

But the poem is perhaps even more striking because of its inspirational as opposed to its doctrinal quality. I have already referred to the mystical configuration implicit in the ideas and images relating to ascent and descent. It is a mystic's experience, too, that is conveyed in the repeated expressions of the need for patience and passivity:

> Déjese descansar de cuando en cuando     175
> sin procurar subir, porque no rompa
> el hilo que el amor queda tramando...
>     Torno a decir que el pecho enamorado
> la celestial, de allá, rica inflüencia
> espere humilde, atento y reposado...     183
>
> (63)

> Así, que el alma en los divinos pechos
> beba infusión de gracia sin buscalla,     215
> sin gana de sentir nuevos provechos,
>     que allí la diligencia menos halla
> cuanto más busca, y suelen los favores
> trocarse en interior, nueva batalla.
>
> (65)

It is only thus that the desired union can be achieved. Such an attitude corresponds to the symbol of the dark night found in the work of San Juan de la Cruz, and echoed in a poem from the present century —in the third part of *East Coker* from T. S. Eliot's *Four Quartets:*

[24] «Francisco de Aldana's Metamorphoses of the Circle», p. 604.

'I said to my soul, be still, and let the dark come upon you
Which shall be the darkness of God. [25]

In these lines, both stillness and darkness are envisaged as a necessary pre-
requisite for eventual illumination, when:

... the darkness shall be the light, and the stillness the dancing.
Whisper of running streams, and winter lightning.
The wild thyme unseen and the wild strawberry...

(p. 28)

In this section Eliot is clearly indebted both to San Juan de la Cruz's *Noche
oscura* and to his prose work, *La subida del Monte Carmelo,* a free and
expanded commentary on the poem. Few mystical utterances can compare
with *Noche oscura* as an expression of joyous intensity when the darkness
and the waiting yield to the explosion of illumination attendant upon union
with God. Yet something of this experience is communicated by Aldana,
both in the poem's climax and, more especially, in the way in which he prepares for it. Though the experience and the vision do not have the sheer
excitement of San Juan's realization, there is no doubting the inspirational
quality of the verse nor the care lavished upon its structure. In this latter
aspect, the use of simile is a dominant and dynamic feature.

Many of the metaphors in the poem relate to specific philosophical and
theological ideas, notably those that allude to the symbol of the sun and the
emblem of the sphere. Indeed the lines that follow the last-quoted description of the soul waiting patiently contain one such image of God's transcendence and immanence:

que el alma, alzada sobre el curso humano,
queda, sin ser curiosa o diligente,
de aquel gran mar cubierta ultramundano,
no, como el pece, sólo exteriormente,
mas dentro mucho más que esté en el fuego          230
el íntimo calor que en él se siente.

(65)

But following this, and to usher in a series of images that prepare for the
poem's climax, there is a simile that is, by contrast, simple and homely:

Digo que, puesta el alma en su sosiego,
espere a Dios cual ojo que cayendo
se va sabrosamente al sueño ciego,
que al que trabaja por quedar durmiendo,          235
esa misma inquietud destrama el hilo
del sueño, que se da no le pidiendo...

(65)

[25] *Four Quartets* (London: Faber and Faber, 1959), p. 27.

This serves the purpose of establishing a base from which the poet can proceed with ever-increasing emotional pace. First comes the river metaphor, suggestive of God's fertility. Notable here is the sonorous assonantal effect of the two verbs in the second line of the *terceto*:

> ella verá con desusado estilo
> toda regarse, y regalarse junto,
> de un salido de Dios sagrado Nilo...                    240
> (66)

The lines that follow express the idea of man's soul as a centre («recogida su luz toda en un punto»), though only an image («imagen y trasunto») of the Centre that is God. But the soul's centre, though distinct from God, is nevertheless, in its state of contemplative union, at one with God:

> y, cual de amor la matutina estrella
> dentro el abismo del eterno día,                    245
> se cubrirá toda luciente y bella.
> (66)

As if aware that, beautiful as this simile is, there can be no definitive expression of such a rarified state, Aldana immediately launches into a simile of Biblical origin, which envisages the soul-God relationship in terms of the bride humbly awaiting the arrival of the bridegroom:

> Como la hermosísima judía
> que, llena de doncel, novicio espanto,
> viendo Isaac que para sí venía,
> dejó cubrir el rostro con el manto                    250
> y, decendida presto del camello,
> recoge humilde al novio casto y santo...
> (66)

This simile derives from the story of Rachel and Isaac rather than from the Song of Solomon, the usual source for the mystical marriage. At this point the recourse to analogy ends, and the poet refers to the inability of words adequately to convey the profound and cherished experience of union. This idea of the inadequacy of language serves ironically as an introduction to the high point of the poem, a passage of considerable rhetorical sweep and power, of which I quote the first part:

> Mas ¿quién dirá, mas quién decir agora
> podrá los peregrinos sentimientos                    260
> que el alma en sus potencias atesora?:
> aquellos ricos amontonamientos
> de sobrecelestiales inflüencias,
> dilatados de amor descubrimientos;

aquellas ilustradas advertencias                    265
de las musas de Dios sobreesenciales,
destierro general de contingencias...

(67)

The high incidence of polysyllabic words here serves to lend these lines an
entirely appropriate majestic air. The passage culminates in the metaphor
of the Indies —a characteristically unexpected touch: [26]

¡Oh grandes, oh riquísimas conquistas
de las Indias de Dios, de aquel gran mundo        275
tan escondido a las ·mundanas vistas!

(67)

In the fifty or so lines that comprise the lead-in to the poem's climax and
the climactic vision itself, what is technically most remarkable, then, is the
variety of metaphor, even to the point of bounteousness. But this is controlled
and shaped in a way that befits the spiritual discipline and divine revelation
described therein. The process is as follows: the idea of light concentrated
(«recogida») in the one point or centre leads to the simile of the morning
star suddenly bedecked by the light of the dawning day; and the concept of
beauty implicit in this figure (the morning star is the planet Venus) leads,
in turn, to the description of Rachel («la hermosísima judía»). This analogy
makes mention of the quality of humility that is necessary for the soul's
union with the Creator, thereby establishing a link with the idea of patient
waiting which had been the starting-point for the whole section. The brilliance of the figurative writing operates within the most logical and coherent
of frameworks.

The final section of the poem is in no sense an anti-climax, especially if
we view it, as I have already suggested, as the final stage in a mystical process. In this connection, moreover, the clear lexical links with the earlier
parts of the poem acquire some significance. For those objects or images
which had previously been a rich source of figurative rationalization (notably the sea and the fish) now operate differently as the most conspicuous
visual elements in the seashore description: what was symbol or analogy
has now become observed reality. By the wealth of detail and by the mode
of description in this final section, the seashore appears as a microcosm,
as a further and, in the context of this particular poem, supreme image of
the Creator's love, in all its variety and energy:

[26] In moral poems of the Golden Age, the Indies are frequently associated with
greed and folly and allied to the Classical idea of the danger associated with sea-voy-
ages. Some writers and poets such as Bartolomé Leonardo de Argensola and Diego de
Saavedra Fajardo saw in the gold of the Indies a cause of Spain's decadence. See
VALENTÍN DE PEDRO, América en las letras españolas del Siglo de Oro (Buenos Aires:
Editorial Sudamericana, 1954), pp. 149-55.

Verás mil retorcidas caracoles,
mil bucíos istriados, con señales
y pintas de lustrosas arreboles:
    los unos del color de los corales,                 385
los otros de la luz que el sol represa
en los pintados arcos celestiales,
    de varia operación, de varia empresa,
despidiendo de sí como centellas,
en rica mezcla de oro y de turquesa.            390
    Cualquiera especie producir de aquéllas
verás (lo que en la tierra no acontece)
pequeñas en estremo y grandes dellas,
    donde el secreto, artificioso pece
pegado está y, en otros, despegarse           395
suele y al mar salir, si le parece;
    por cierto, cosa digna de admirarse
tan menudo animal sin niervo y hueso
encima tan gran máquina arrastrarse...

(71-72)

The notion of the seashore and its teeming life as a microcosm is enhanced by terminology suggestive of cosmic functions: the shellfish and whelks are not only innumerable and brilliant but also varied in their activities, contributing to the richness and efficiency of the little world: «de varia operación, de varia empresa». It is significant too when the poet speaks of the different kinds of shells that he draws particular attention to the extremes of size that he perceives in them; in such a line as «pequeñas en estremo y grandes dellas», with its clear antithesis of the small and the large, he reveals perhaps his intuition of the world as reflection and microcosm. In a description of his wonder at how the flimsy creature within the shell («tan menudo animal sin niervo y hueso») can drag along its comparatively weighty encumbrance, Aldana employs a term that may seem unusual here —«máquina»— but which has more far-reaching associations, even of cosmic significance.[27] Indeed, it is possible that in the all but unobserved behaviour and movements of the creature within the shell, which he describes as «el secreto, artificioso pece», the poet finds an analogy for the conditions for his own soul's spiritual movement —equally imperceptible to outer gaze but inwardly equally sure— that has been the poem's principal concern.

Towards the end there is a broadening of the vision: the poet's eyes focus on the movement of the waves in a choppy sea and the progress of a ship that sails off to distant lands: «la nave, a lejos climas peregrina» (72). Some three hundred lines earlier, the poet had spoken of how his own ship —a symbol of his spiritual quest— was setting off on its own journey of exploration:

[27] Compare for instance Góngora's reference to the sky as «estrellada máquina luciente» in his *Panegírico al Duque de Lerma;* and Quevedo's phrase «universal máquina» in one of his love sonnets (*ed. cit.,* p. 362).

Mas pues, Montano, va mi navecilla
corriendo este gran mar con suelta vela
hacia la infinidad buscando orilla... 125

(61)

There is, finally, a reference to the sea itself in one of its calm moods («mansa y reposada»). The reference to the sea's music («música voz, süave y pura») brings to mind the idea of the music of the spheres, the divine harmony that sustains the universe. This is a parallel that is suggested both by the poet's treatment of seashore life as a microcosm and by the predominant Neoplatonic flavour of the poem's ideas and attitude. There follow a few lines by way of valediction and the poem —probably Aldana's last— ends with the date of its completion: «a los siete de setiembre, / mil y quinientos y setenta y siete» (74).

This year —1577— may well have been an *annus mirabilis* for Spanish religious and philosophical poetry. Apart from the *Carta para Arias Montano,* it seems certain that in this same year San Juan de la Cruz wrote of his mystical experience during his imprisonment in Toledo and it is likely that Fray Luis de León was engaged on some of his greatest poems. In any case, the late 1570s certainly represent the summit of Spanish religious verse. Aldana's poem to Arias Montano shares common ground with both his distinguished contemporaries: the other-worldly aspiration and philosophical premises of Fray Luis and the inspirational yet schematized understanding of experience of San Juan. But for the final principal section of the poem —the seashore description— there is no obvious literary precedent, certainly not in Spanish poetry. Indeed for the sense of detail arising from an almost scientific curiosity, we have to look further afield. The name that comes to mind is Leonardo da Vinci —a Florentine, as was Aldana, at least by his upbringing and intellectual and cultural formation. In the painstaking detail of many of Leonardo's drawings of plants and animals —especially horses— there is a parallel for Aldana's feeling of wonder and intensity of interest in his seashore description. [28] Seldom can a poem of such philosophical import have concluded so felicitously and in so relaxed a fashion. The concentration demanded by the rigorously apt figurative writing for two-thirds of the work is apparently released by the sense of visual immediacy and discovery in the last, lingering scene.

But perhaps the abiding impression of this work is its humility. This becomes all the more striking if we recall that in the same year Aldana had

[28] There are also notable descriptions of horses in Aldana's verse. See, for example, the three stanzas beginning «Tiembla el Cauallo altivo, y generoso» in *Otavas sobre diversas materias* (OC, II, 154-55); and the passage describing the four horses that draw Apollo's chariot in the *Fábula de Faetonte* (OC, I, 175-76). In *Medoro y Angélica,* the neighing of horses is suggested in a splendidly alliterative line («hinchían de relinchos todo el cielo») that repeats a phrase found in the *Fábula de Faetone* («Hinchiendo de relinchos todo el cielo»).

written the inflated, cliché-ridden *Otavas dirigidas al rey don Felipe* with its strident nationalism. A year later, indeed, Aldana was to die alongside King Sebastian at Alcazarquivir. A contemporary account based on information received from survivors of the battle mentions Aldana's bravery: «Y con la espada en la mano tinta en sangre se metió entre los enemigos, haziendo el oficio de tan buen soldado y capitán como él era.» [29] Indeed for many years after, the disaster continued to attract writers, and in a number of plays, among them Lope de Vega's *Tragedia del Rey don Sebastián y bautismo del príncipe de Marruecos,* Aldana figures as a noble hero. [30] There is no reason for questioning this idealization of the dead poet. Nor do the folly of the enterprise and the fanaticism that inspired it detract from the courage of the «divino capitán»; we can admire the warrior even if we object to the cause or, more precisely, —the manner in which that cause was pursued. But it is the man of letters —the poet— that posterity has recognized, without whom the soldier would have been no more than a forgotten dot on the map of history. It is, above all, the poet who, by observation and meditation, came humbly to understand the value of all created things. In this Neoplatonic epistle, his poetic testament, he bequeathed a simple and noble truth:

y sienta que la mano dadivosa           160
de Dios cosas crïó tantas y tales,
hasta la más süez, mínima cosa...
    Enamórese el alma en ver cuán bueno
es Dios, que un gusanillo le podría        170
llamar su crïador de lleno en lleno.

(63)

---

[29] This extract from an account by Diego de Torres is printed in RIVERS, *Francisco de Aldana, el Divino Capitán,* p. 120. Portuguese historians, eager to defend the reputation and the myth of King Sebastian, have tended to make something of a scapegoat of Aldana. See RUIZ SILVA, *Estudios sobre Francisco de Aldana,* p. 17n.
[30] *Ibid.,* pp. 51-60.

# LIST OF WORKS CONSULTED

### EDITIONS OF ALDANA'S POETRY

*Primera parte de las obras, que hasta agora se han podido hallar del Capitan Francisco de Aldana, Alcayde de San Sebastian, el qual murio peleando en la jornada de Africa...* (Milán: Pablo Gotardo Poncio, [1589]).

*Segunda parte de las obras, que se han podido hallar del Capitan Francisco de Aldana, Alcayde de San Sebastian, que fué Maestre de Campo General del Rey de Portugal, en la jornada de Africa, adonde murio peleando...* (Madrid: P. Madrigal, 1591).

*Todas las obras que hasta agora se han podido hallar del Capitán Francisco de Aldana, Alcayde de San Sebastián, que fué Maestro de Campo General del Rey de Portugal en la jornada de Africa, a do murió peleando...* (Madrid: Luys Sánchez, 1593).

*Obras completas,* 2 vols., ed. Manuel Moragón Mestre (Madrid: Consejo Superior de Investigaciones Científicas, 1953).

*Poesías,* ed. Elías L. Rivers (Madrid: Clásicos Castellanos, 1957).

*Epistolario poético completo,* ed. Antonio Rodríguez-Moñino (Madrid: Turner, 1978).

*Poesías castellanas completas,* ed. José Lara Garrido (Madrid: Cátedra, 1985).

### BOOKS AND ARTICLES ON ALDANA

CERNUDA, LUIS: «Tres poetas metafísicos», *Bulletin of Spanish Studies,* 25 (1948), 109-18.

CRAWFORD, J. P. W.: «Francisco de Aldana: A Neglected Poet of the Golden Age in Spain», *Hispanic Review,* 7 (1939), 48-61.

FERRATÉ, JUAN: «Siete sonetos de Francisco de Aldana», in *Teoría del poema* (Barcelona: Seix Barral, 1957), pp. 69-80.

————: «Una muestra de poesía extravagante. Las octavas sobre los *Efectos de Amor* de Francisco de Aldana», in *Dinámica de la poesía* (Barcelona: Seix Barral, 1968), pp. 215-43.

GREEN, OTIS H.: «On Francisco de Aldana: Observations on Dr. Rivers' Study of El Divino Capitán», *Hispanic Review,* 26 (1958), 117-35.

————: «A Wedding *Introito* by Francisco de Aldana (1537-1578)», *Hispanic Review,* 31 (1963), 8-21.

LEFEBVRE, ALFREDO: *La poesía del capitán Aldana (1537-1578)* (Concepción: Universidad de Concepción, 1953).

LONGFELLOW, HENRY W.: «Spanish Devotional and Moral Poetry», *North American Review,* 34, n.º 75 (April, 1832), 277-315.

RIVERS, ELÍAS L.: «A New Manuscript of a Poem hitherto attributed to Fray Luis de León», *Hispanic Review,* 20 (1952), 153-58.

————: «New Biographical Data on Francisco de Aldana», *Romanic Review*, 44 (1953). 166-84.

————: *Francisco de Aldana: el Divino Capitán* (Badajoz: Institución de Servicios Culturales, 1955).

RUIZ SILVA, CARLOS: *Estudios sobre Francisco de Aldana* (Valladolid: Universidad de Valladolid, 1981).

SALSTAD, M. LOUISE: «Francisco de Aldana's Metamorphoses of the Circle», *Modern Language Review*, 74 (1979), 599-606.

TERRY, ARTHUR: «Thought and Feeling in Three Golden Age Sonnets», *Bulletin of Hispanic Studies*, 59 (1982), 237-46.

WALTERS, D. GARETH: «On the Text, Source and Significance of Aldana's *Medoro y Angélica*», *Forum for Modern Language Studies*, 20 (1984), 17-29.


OTHER WORKS CITED AND CONSULTED

ACUÑA, HERNANDO DE: *Varias poesías*, ed. Luis F. Díaz Larios (Madrid: Cátedra, 1982).

ALZIEU, PIERRE, JAMMES, ROBERT AND LISSORGUES, YVAN: *Poesía erótica del Siglo de Oro* (Barcelona: Editorial Crítica, 1984).

ARISTOTLE: *The Nicomachean Ethics*, translated with commentaries and glossary by Hippocrates G. Apostle (Dordrecht: D. Reidel, 1975).

CALDERÓN DE LA BARCA, PEDRO: *No hay más fortuna que Dios*, ed. A. A. Parker (Manchester: Manchester University Press, 1962).

CAMÕES, LUÍS DE: *Obras completas I*, ed. Hernâni Cidade, 3rd edn (Lisbon: Sá da Costa, 1962).

CHEVALIER, MAXIME: *Los temas ariostescos en el romancero y la poesía española del siglo de oro* (Madrid: Castalia, 1968).

COHEN, J. M. (ed.): *The Penguin Book of Spanish Verse* (Harmondsworth: Penguin Books, 1960).

COSSÍO, J. M.: *Fábulas mitológicas en España* (Madrid: Espasa-Calpe, 1952).

CUEVAS, CRISTÓBAL (ed.): *Fray Luis de León y la escuela salmantina* (Madrid: Taurus, 1982).

DAVIES, STEVIE: *Renaissance Views of Man* (Manchester: Manchester University Press, 1978).

ELIOT, T. S.: *Four Quartets* (London: Faber and Faber, 1959).

ELLIOTT, J. H.: *Imperial Spain 1469-1716* (Harmondsworth: Penguin Books, 1970).

FERRONI, GIULIO (ed.): *Poesia italiana del Cinquecento* (Milan: Garzanti, 1978).

FICINO, MARSILIO: *Commentary on Plato's* Symposium, translated by Sears Reynolds Jayne (Columbia: University of Missouri, 1944).

FORSTER, LEONARD: *The Icy Fire. Five Studies in European Petrarchism* (Cambridge: Cambridge University Press, 1969).

FUCILLA, J. G.: *Estudios sobre el petrarquismo en España* (Madrid: Consejo Superior de Investigaciones Científicas, 1960).

GARCILASO DE LA VEGA: *Poesías castellanas completas*, ed. E. L. Rivers, 2nd edn (Madrid: Castalia, 1972).

GARDNER, HELEN (ed.): *The Metaphysical Poets*, 2nd edn (Harmondsworth: Penguin Books, 1966).

GICOVATE, BERNARD (ed.): *Garcilaso y su escuela poética* (Madrid: Taurus, 1983).

GIL POLO, GASPAR: *Diana enamorada*, ed. Rafael Ferreres, Clásicos Castellanos (Madrid: Espasa-Calpe, 1962).

GÓNGORA, LUIS DE: *Sonetos completos*, ed. Biruté Ciplijauskaité, 3rd edn (Madrid: Castalia, 1978).

————: *Romances*, ed. Antonio Carreño (Madrid: Cátedra, 1982).

GREEN, OTIS H.: *Spain and the Western Tradition. The Castilian Mind in Literature from El Cid to Calderón,* 4 vols. (Madison, Milwaukee and London: University of Wisconsin Press, 1968).

JONES, R. O.: *A Literary History of Spain. The Golden Age: Prose and Poetry* (London: Ernest Benn, 1971).

JUAN DE LA CRUZ, SAN: *Vida y obras de San Juan de la Cruz,* biography by P. Crisógono de Jesús, revised by P. Matías del Niño Jesús, edition of works by P. Lucinio del SS. Sacramento, 4th edn (Madrid: Biblioteca de Autores Cristianos, 1960).

KENISTON, HAYWARD: *Garcilaso de la Vega: A Critical Study of his Life and Works* (New York: Hispanic Society of America, 1922).

KRAILSHEIMER, A. J. (ed.): *The Continental Renaissance* (Harmondsworth: Penguin Books, 1971).

KRISTELLER, PAUL O.: *Renaissance Thought. The Classic, Scholastic and Humanist Strains* (New York: Harper Torchbooks, 1961).

LAPESA, RAFAEL: «El hipérbaton en la poesía de Fray Luis de León», in *Studies in Spanish Literature of the Golden Age Presented to Edward M. Wilson,* ed. R. O. Jones (London: Tamesis Books, 1973), pp. 137-47.

LEÓN, FRAY LUIS DE: *Poesías,* ed. Oreste Macrí (Barcelona: Editorial Crítica, 1982).

MCNERNEY, KATHLEEN: *The Influence of Ausiàs March on Early Golden Age Poetry* (Amsterdam: Editions Rodopi B. V., 1982).

PARKER, A. A.: *The Philosophy of Love in Spanish Literature 1480-1680,* ed. T. O'Reilly (Edinburgh: Edinburgh University Press, 1985).

PEDRO, VALENTÍN DE: *América en las letras españolas del Siglo de Oro* (Buenos Aires: Editorial Sudamericana, 1954).

PETRARCA, FRANCESCO: *Canzoniere,* ed. Dino Provenzal (Milan: Rizzoli, 1954).

QUEVEDO, FRANCISCO DE: *Obras completas. Obras en verso,* ed. L. Astrana Marín (Madrid: Aguilar, 1934).

———: *Obras completas I. Poesía original,* ed. J. M. Blecua, 2nd. edn (Barcelona: Planeta, 1968).

———: *Sueños y discursos,* ed. Felipe C. R. Maldonado (Madrid: Castalia, 1972).

———: *Poesía varia,* ed. J. O. Crosby (Madrid: Cátedra, 1981).

REICHENBERGER, ARNOLD: «Boscan's *Epístola a Mendoza*», *Hispanic Review,* 17 (1949), 1-17.

RIVERS, ELÍAS L.: «The Horatian Epistle and its Introduction into Spanish Literature». *Hispanic Review,* 22 (1954), 175-94.

TERRY, ARTHUR (ed.): *An Anthology of Spanish Poetry 1500-1700. Part One: 1500-1580* (Oxford: Pergamon, 1965).

TORRE, FRANCISCO DE LA: *Poesías,* ed. Alonso Zamora Vicente, Clásicos Castellanos (Madrid: Espasa-Calpe, 1969).

VEGA CARPIO, LOPE DE: *Rimas de Tomé de Burguillos,* ed. J. M. Blecua (Barcelona: Planeta, 1976).

VILLAMEDIANA, CONDE DE: *Obras,* ed. J. M. Rozas (Madrid: Castalia, 1969).

WALTERS, D. GARETH: «Three Examples of Petrarchism in Quevedo's *Heráclito cristiano*», *Bulletin of Hispanic Studies,* 58 (1981), 21-30.

———: *Francisco de Quevedo, Love Poet* (Washington and Cardiff: CUA Press and University of Wales Press, 1985).

———: «On the Structure, Imagery and Significance of *Vida retirada*», *Modern Language Review,* 81 (1986), 71-81.

WHINNOM, KEITH: *La poesía amatoria de la época de los Reyes Católicos* (Durham: University of Durham, 1981).

WILKINS, E. H.: *A History of Italian Literature* (Cambridge, Massachusetts: Harvard University Press, 1974).